MICROWORLDS ADVENTURES WITH LOGO

Richard Noss · Clare Smallman · Michael Thorne

Hutchinson

London Melbourne Sydney Auckland Johannesburg

About this book

Why we wrote a book of LOGO ideas

LOGO is the first of a new generation of computer languages. It is the first of a new generation of computer languages. It is a powerful language designed for learning, which offers an unprecedented range of creative possibilities.

This book is not a tutorial, it is a book of ideas. It is the ideas, not the finished programs which are important. Learning LOGO is like learning any language. The best way is to immerse yourself in it, even if, to begin with, it's hard to understand every word.

Rather than having a particular age-group in mind, this book was designed to appeal to the whole family. We hope that young learners will find much of the book exciting, but there is plenty of material to stimulate the imagination of older readers – including adults!

The creative potential of LOGO stems from its capabilities as a tool for modelling the structures and patterns of our surroundings. It is an old saying that we don't really understand something until we've taught it to someone else. Programming in LOGO helps you understand how things work.

How to use this book

Our aim in this book is to suggest some of the ways in which the power of the LOGO language can be realized by all. It consists of a series of 'Microworlds' arranged in double-page spreads. Microworlds are mini-environments for exploring ideas. They are catalysts for thinking and learning.

There is no need to work through this book in order. We will feel much more successful if we tempt you into dodging between the microworlds. The only pages which we suggest you read are those in which the characters in the book are introduced (pages 4 and 5).

We have assumed that you will have access to the LOGO manual which applies to your particular computer system – they are all slightly different. The LOGO version on which this book is based can be used more or less as it stands with systems like the Sinclair Spectrum, Atari, Apple LOGO, and at least two of the versions available for the BBC computer.

There is another resource that we hope you will have – other people. It may seem strange at first to think of programming as a social activity involving the communication of thoughts and the expression of ideas, rather than typing obscure code. We hope that LOGO will change your mind.

Richard Noss
Clare Smallman
Michael Thorne

To Joseph, Jonathon, Vicki and James

Hutchinson and Co. (Publishers) Ltd
An imprint of the Hutchinson Publishing Group
17-21 Conway Street, London W1P 6JD

Hutchinson Publishing Group (Australia) Pty Ltd
16-22 Church Street, Hawthorn, Melbourne, Victoria 3122

Hutchinson Group (NZ) Ltd
32-34 View Road, PO Box 40-086, Glenfield, Auckland 10

Hutchinson Group (SA) (Pty) Ltd
PO Box 337, Bergvlei 2012, South Africa

First published 1985 by Hutchinson and Co. (Publishers) Ltd
in association with Thames Television International Ltd,
149 Tottenham Court Road, London W1P 9LL

Designed by The Pen & Ink Book Company Ltd
Typeset in 14 on 16pt Quorum Book by The Pen & Ink Book Company Ltd
Illustrations by John Higgins and The Pen & Ink Book Company Ltd

British Library Cataloguing in Publication Data
Noss, Richard
    Microworlds : adventures with LOGO.
    1. LOGO (Computer program language) – Juvenile
literature
    I. Title II. Smallman, Clare III. Thorne, Michael
    0001.64'24   QA76.73.L63

ISBN 0 09 1611111 3

Printed at The Bath Press, Avon

Contents

Introduction

Turtle search

Turtle search is a version of Battleships.
You need: 2 grids and a cut out turtle each.
To play:

1. Each player draws 1 pen, 3 toffees and 4 carrots on one grid.
2. Place your turtle on your blank grid. Turtles start in the bottom left hand corner.
3. Take it in turns to call out moves for the turtles. Use forward, back, right turn and left turn. When you move forward and back you must say how much. The dotted line shows

    FORWARD 2
    TURNRIGHT
    FORWARD 2

4. When you find part of a pen, toffee or carrot, mark it on your blank grid.

Trace me

Um, maybe if I go back 1, turn left and forward 3, I'll get...

Turtle golf

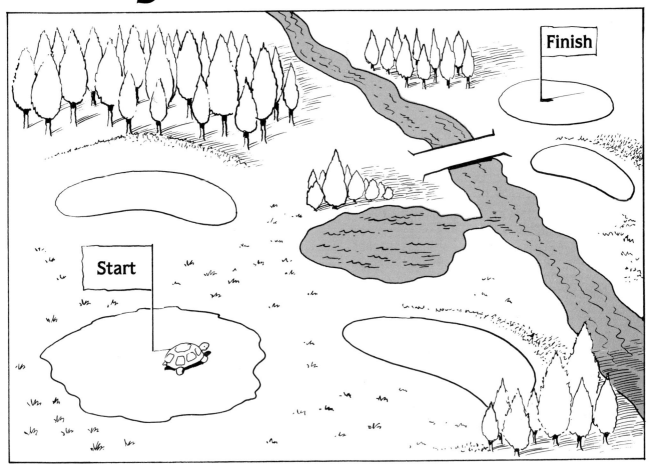

Draw a golf course on a large sheet of paper. Stand the floor turtle at the start and try to get to the finishing hole in as few moves as you can. If you haven't got a floor turtle, draw the golf course on an acetate sheet and stick it over the screen. When you turn or move the turtle, you always say how much.

You'll have to work out the exact rules yourself.

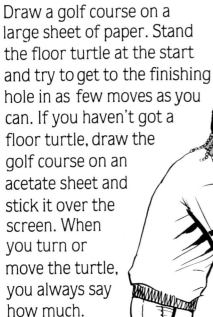

So if it goes into the wood that loses me one move. I think the pond counts as losing 2.

I vote the turtle's only in the hole if it isn't touching the sides at all.

Up and down

The turtle loves toffee — but has to get to the sweet shop without leaving a tell tale line across 'NO TURTLES' land. PENUP (or PU) and PENDOWN (or PD) can help — try them with a version of the map drawn on a transparent sheet for a screen turtle or a large piece of paper for the floor turtle.

If you are drawing on a screen, you can rub out a line if you make a mistake. Type PE or PENERASE and find out how it works. If your computer says I DONT KNOW HOW TO PE look in your LOGO manual for the right command. You'll need to find out how to switch off PENERASE.

The turtle drew this sign. Could you draw one?

Turtle games

A game for lots of people

1. Sit in a circle.
2. Draw a small circle (make sure you can rub it out!) big enough for someone to sit in.
3. Choose someone to sit in the small circle.
4. Choose a 'turtle' and blindfold him or her.
5. Turn the turtle round a few times to confuse them.
6. The 'turtle' has to find the sitting person following LOGO commands given by everyone else. The turtle has to obey them exactly.
7. When the turtle finds the person in the ring, the person who gave the last LOGO command is the next turtle.
8. The old turtle is the new person sitting in the ring.

And a game for 2 people and a computer

1. One person draws a picture on the screen.
2. The other person, who has a sheet of paper and a pencil, does not see the screen.
3. As the first person draws with the computer, they call out the commands.
4. The second person draws what they think the turtle will do.
5. When the picture is finished, the second person guesses what it is.

Take home a turtle

You can clear the screen by typing **CLEARSCREEN** or **CS** or **DRAW** (it depends on your version of LOGO). When you do you send the turtle to its **home** position.

If you want to send the turtle home without clearing the screen, use **HOME**. Try these:

```
FD  61     LT  100  FD  56        PD  FD  50  HOME
RT  57     RT  210  FD  58        RT  30  FD  52  HOME
FD  40     PU                     LT  30  FD  50  HOME
HOME       HOME
```

When you type **HOME**, LOGO sends the turtle back to the middle of the screen and sets it back to its 'home' heading — pointing straight up.

Try this — **FENCE**
          FD 1000

You will probably get a message like **TURTLE OUT OF BOUNDS.**

Typing **FENCE** stops the turtle going beyond the edge of the screen.

Fence

Window

Wrap

Find the turtle

Send the turtle on a journey round the screen by typing something like **WINDOW FD 2000 RT 100 FD 2000** Where will the turtle come from when you type **HOME**? The person who guesses closest is the winner.

Turtle town

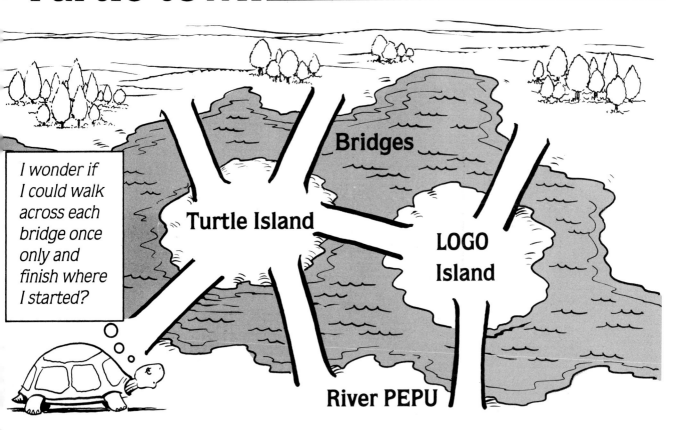

I wonder if I could walk across each bridge once only and finish where I started?

Bridges

Turtle Island

LOGO Island

River PEPU

Turtle slalom

Turtle slalom tracks can be built from all sorts of things and you can use a screen turtle too. The game is to get round in as few moves as possible.

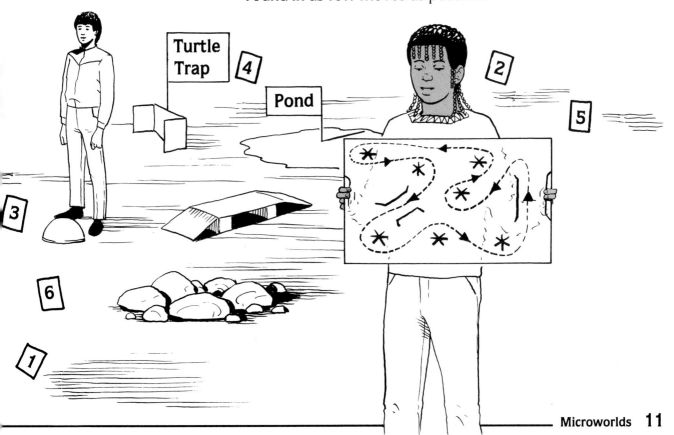

Turtle Trap

Pond

Playing turtle

Playing turtle can help you get your LOGO commands right.

Draw in sand.

Draw on paper.

Playing turtle is good for sorting out bugs. When things don't turn out the way you expect, you've got a bug.

I always get my left and right mixed up.

You mean left this time.

Move yourself.

It's forward a bit and turn a bit.

Or just walk.

Ogol and Orcim play turtle in their heads.

LOGO eyes

is playing turtle in
your head.

Again and again

In the picture many patterns are REPEATed. If you want to do something again and again in LOGO, use the LOGO word REPEAT. REPEAT works like this

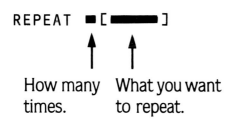

How many times.   What you want to repeat.

Try these

REPEAT 3[FD 50 RT 60]

REPEAT 50[FD 10 BK 10 RT 2]

RT 4 REPEAT 200 [PU FD 100 PD BK

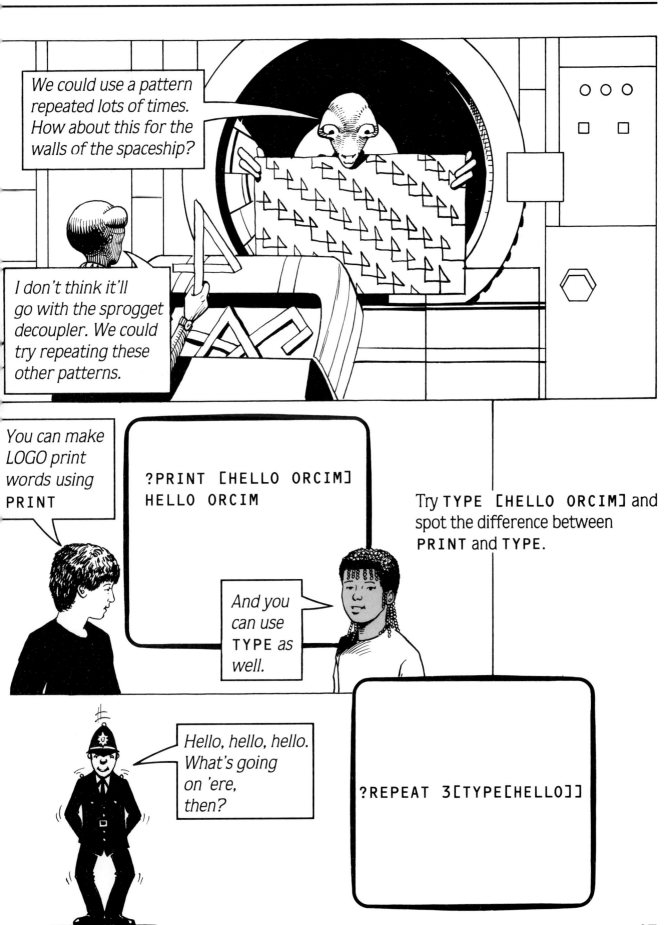

We could use a pattern repeated lots of times. How about this for the walls of the spaceship?

I don't think it'll go with the sprogget decoupler. We could try repeating these other patterns.

You can make LOGO print words using PRINT

```
?PRINT [HELLO ORCIM]
HELLO ORCIM
```

And you can use TYPE as well.

Try TYPE [HELLO ORCIM] and spot the difference between PRINT and TYPE.

Hello, hello, hello. What's going on 'ere, then?

```
?REPEAT 3[TYPE[HELLO]]
```

Round and round

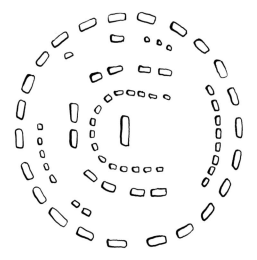

Stonehenge on Salisbury Plain is sometimes called a stone circle. The plan on the left shows how the stones were or are arranged.

What's this shape? Join up the dots. It may give you some ideas if you want to draw a circle with the turtle.

23   22
24   •21   44   45
    •20 •43   •46
25•
    11   28 19 30   31   47   59
26   10   29 42   32   61 60
1   (PU)•   9   27   •41
12   (PD)•   •58
        •8   •18   33• 62   •48
2 •   40 (PD)   50 63
    13   15 16 •17   51 (PU) 34 49   •57
    14 7 39 (PU)
        •38
3 •   •35   •52 (PD)   56
    •6   •37
                36   53 55
4   •5   54

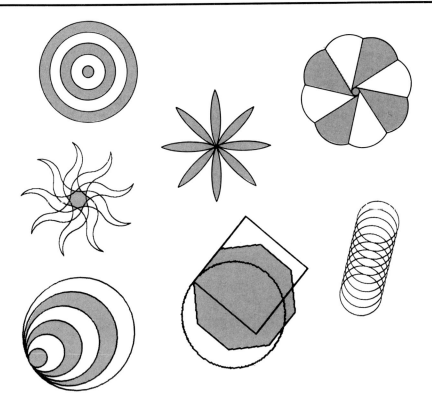

Your version of LOGO may have **ARCR** and **ARCL** which will make drawing shapes with curves easier.
If you do have these commands explore how they work.

When stuck, play turtle by walking your procedure or the shape you want.

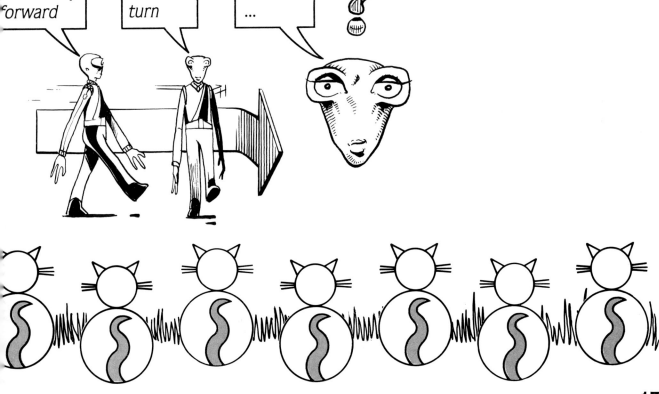

Take a step forward

and then turn

and then ...

Strange flowers

I think I can draw a triangle.

I'm working on a square.

I can do 6 sides. I found it by accident trying to draw a triangle.

The problem is to know how much to turn.

Using REPEAT *to find an angle*

Jeff and Jane drew a 5 sided shape using REPEAT to try out the angles.

They used HIDETURTLE (or HT to check their shape was closed

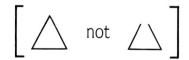

```
REPEAT 5[FD 30 RT 125]
REPEAT 5[FD 30 RT 50]
REPEAT 5[FD 30 RT 110]
REPEAT 5[FD 30 RT 70]
REPEAT [FD 30 RT 85]
        oops↗
REPEAT 5[FD 30 RT 85]
```

Are they getting closer?

If we knew how many REPEATs there are, I think we could work out the angle to make it close.

And if we knew the angle maybe we could work out the number of REPEATs.

```
REPEAT? [FD RT?]
```

What's the link?

LOGO can do your arithmetic for you.
```
PRINT 10+10
PRINT 5*4
PRINT 1+2+3+4+5+6+7+8+9+10
```

Can it divide and take away as well? And do you need to put PRINT ?

?PRINT 10/12

FD 50+50
RT 2*10

Dunno — we can try.

Strange flowers can be made by REPEATing doodles.

```
REPEAT 100 [FD 72 RT 130 FD 56]
REPEAT 500[   ]
```

Your own commands

Beginning and ending

Try FORWARD 30!

I keep getting lost.

Make a list of what you want to do first — like a recipe.

A recipe is just a list of things to do. Here's how to make Orcim's favourite chocolate biscuits.

Ingredients

100 g margarine
200 g sugar
200 g self raising flour
½ tsp baking powder
½ tsp salt
1 egg (beaten)
50 g chocolate

TO COOK BISCUITS

Melt the margarine in a saucepan and remove it from the heat.
Weigh the sugar and stir into the margarine.
Chop the chocolate into small pieces and stir into the flour.
Stir the flour and chocolate into the saucepan.
Add salt and beaten egg.
Put small balls of the mixture on a greased baking tray (well spaced out as they spread).
Cook at Gas 4 or 350°F. Take them out of the oven before they brown if you want them really chewy. Take them off the tray when they're cool.
END

It's not very like a spaceship. May be you missed something out.

A SPACESHIP

Well yes, there was a bug, but we liked it, so we kept it.

Getting up list

Put on underpants
put on jeans
put on socks
put on shoes
put on T-shirt
drink tea

Ogol followed his getting up list and lost his pyjamas. And what happened to them? Find the bug in Ogol's getting up procedure.

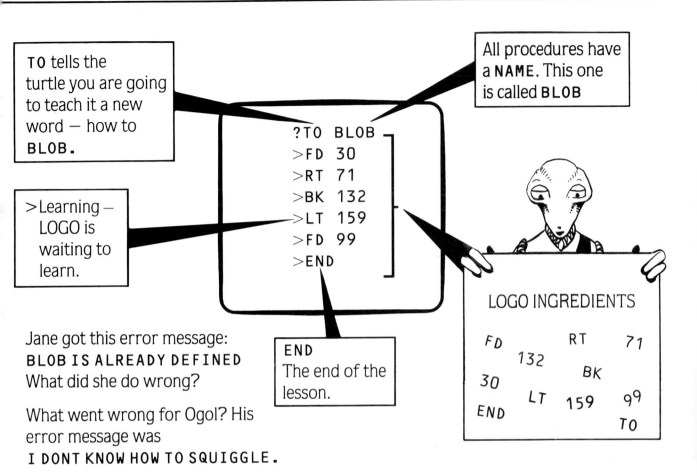

TO tells the turtle you are going to teach it a new word — how to **BLOB**.

All procedures have a **NAME**. This one is called **BLOB**

```
?TO  BLOB
>FD  30
>RT  71
>BK  132
>LT  159
>FD  99
>END
```

>Learning —
LOGO is waiting to learn.

END
The end of the lesson.

LOGO INGREDIENTS

FD   RT   71
      132   BK
30   LT 159   99
END   TO

Jane got this error message:
BLOB IS ALREADY DEFINED
What did she do wrong?

What went wrong for Ogol? His error message was
I DONT KNOW HOW TO SQUIGGLE.

Jane gave this puzzle to Orcim. What procedure did Jane use to give the answers?

SWAN	S
OTTER	T
CROCODILE	O
BEAR	R
BLACKBIRD	K

Okay. My turn. What was the procedure for this?

?SHAPE

?Doing —
LOGO is waiting to do something.

Teaching turtles

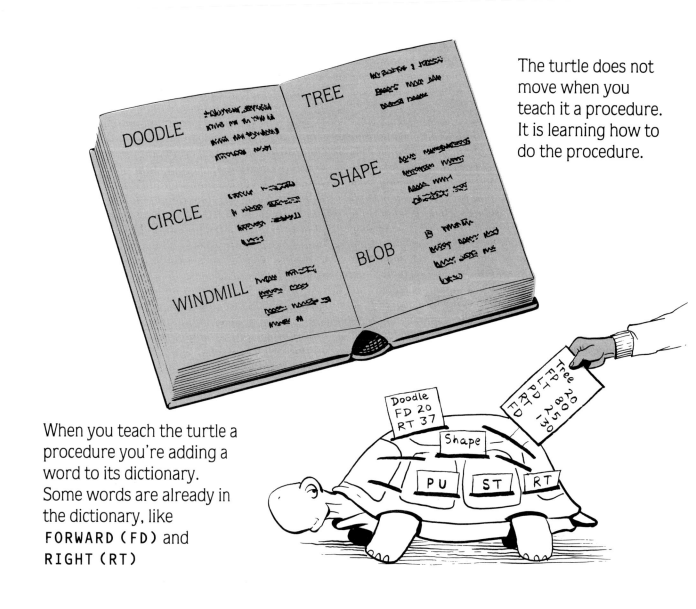

The turtle does not move when you teach it a procedure. It is learning how to do the procedure.

When you teach the turtle a procedure you're adding a word to its dictionary. Some words are already in the dictionary, like FORWARD (FD) and RIGHT (RT)

When you want to use a procedure, type the procedure's name. The turtle finds the name in its dictionary and off it goes. It won't mind how many times you ask it to do the procedure.

Jeff drew a tree by typing out one command at a time. He used his LOGO eyes as he went along. His commands started like this:

```
FD 20
FD 5
RT 70
RT 50
RT 20
LT 10
```

He could have saved some time. How?

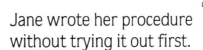

Jane wrote her procedure without trying it out first.

```
TO CRACKER
.
.
.
.
PD 10
END
```

Unlike Jeff, she planned her procedure on paper, Which way suits you?

Twinkle twinkle

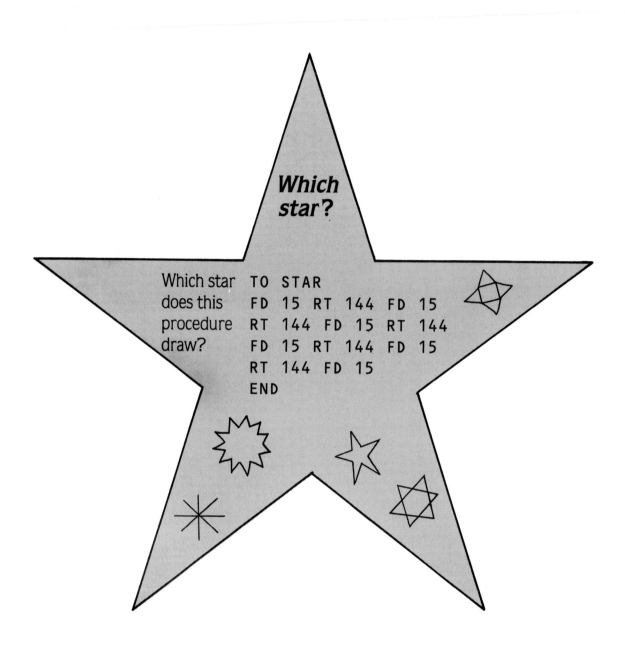

Which star?

Which star does this procedure draw?

```
TO STAR
FD 15 RT 144 FD 15
RT 144 FD 15 RT 144
FD 15 RT 144 FD 15
RT 144 FD 15
END
```

Some stars come in pairs. They are called binaries. Choose your own starshape and write a procedure to draw binary stars.

?BINARY STARS

Some stars are so far away they just twinkle. A distant star might look like this.

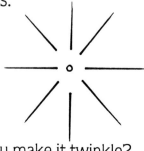

Can you make it twinkle?

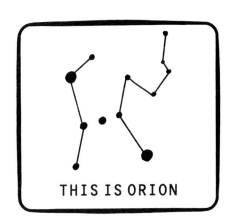

THIS IS ORION

You can label your picture using
PRINT.
PRINT [THIS IS ORION]

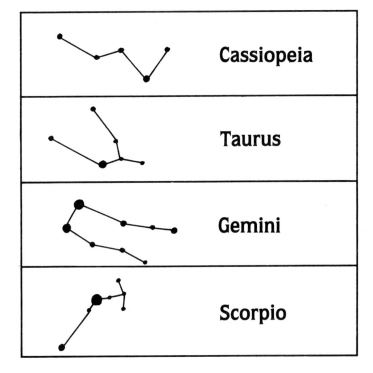

Cassiopeia

Taurus

Gemini

Scorpio

Turtle getting in the way? Making a mess on the screen? You need HIDETURTLE (or HT), SHOWTURTLE (or ST) or CLEARSCREEN (or CS).

Can you move your label and put it next to the star pattern? This is only possible with some versions of LOGO.

Treetops

EDIT tells LOGO that you want to change a procedure. The editor in LOGO helps you to make changes and correct mistakes. When you type

    EDIT "NEWTREE

LOGO displays the procedure **NEWTREE.** Usually there is a message like **LOGO EDITOR** on the screen to remind you that now you can change your procedure.

```
?TO NEWTREE
>FD 50
>RT 40
>FD 50
>RT 40
>FD 50
>RT 40
>FD 50
>RT 40
>FD 50
>RT 40
>END
```

LOGO EDITOR

3 things you might like to do with the editor.

Rub out a whole line with one key press.

Get out of the editor without changing your procedure (in case case you get in a mess).

There are lots of keys to help you edit procedures. Each computer has different ones, so you'll need to look at your LOGO manual to find out exactly what to press.

Move the cursor (the flashing square) around the screen using the keys marked

and

Find which key rubs out (it may be called DELETE). You also need to know how to get out of the editor.

TIP ONE
Stick with the keys you know already until you are happy with them.

TIP TWO
When you need to know more editing tricks, ask a friend (or use your LOGO manual).

Make space for a whole new line.

Snail trail

What animal carries its house on its back Ogol?

I don't know, but it must be big to carry a house.

A snail. It has a squiggly shell that goes round and inside itself.

It gets bigger and goes round itself.

?SNAIL
?

Like this?

You wrote lots of procedures. It must have taken ages.

Not if you edit the name

like this.

```
TO TRIANGLE 4
FD 10 25
RT 120
FD 10 25
RT 120
FD 10 25
RT 120
END
```

It's nice but it still doesn't look like a snail.

?SNAIL

No it twists round.

No all the bits join up in a line.

Why didn't you say so?

?SNAIL2

Go along... turn a bit... go along a bit... turn a bit.

Pretty, b the corn are too sharp.

Still too sharp.

Nearly – try maki the leng shorter do a few more tu

That's a very square snail.

Loading and saving

Jane

Jeff

I'm going to keep this somewhere safe.

When you switch off your computer, it forgets everything you've taught it — it loses everything from its memory. If you want to keep your procedures, you'll need to save them. You can do this on a cassette tape, or on a disk — it depends which you have. When you switch on again, you can load your procedures from the tape or disk into the computer's memory. Look in your manual for details of saving and loading (or ask a friend).

Aaghhh, I've lost my copy. Let me borrow your copy. I'll load it onto the computer and then save it onto blank tape.

Lucky I saved it.

SCRATCN

Nose about

At the centre of everyone's face is a nose.
The two halves of a nose are the same.

Lots of things are like this.

```
TO PUZZLE1
LT 90
FD 50
RT 60
FD 20
RT 120
FD 70
LT 90
FD 40
LT 130
FD 50
LT 140
FD 40
END
```

Swap all the LT commands for RT commands and RT commands for LT to produce PUZZLE2.
Try
```
CS
PUZZLE1
PUZZLE
```
Make PUZZLE3 from PUZZLE1 by swapping every FD for a BK and every BK for a FD.

Try the same trick on your own procedures.

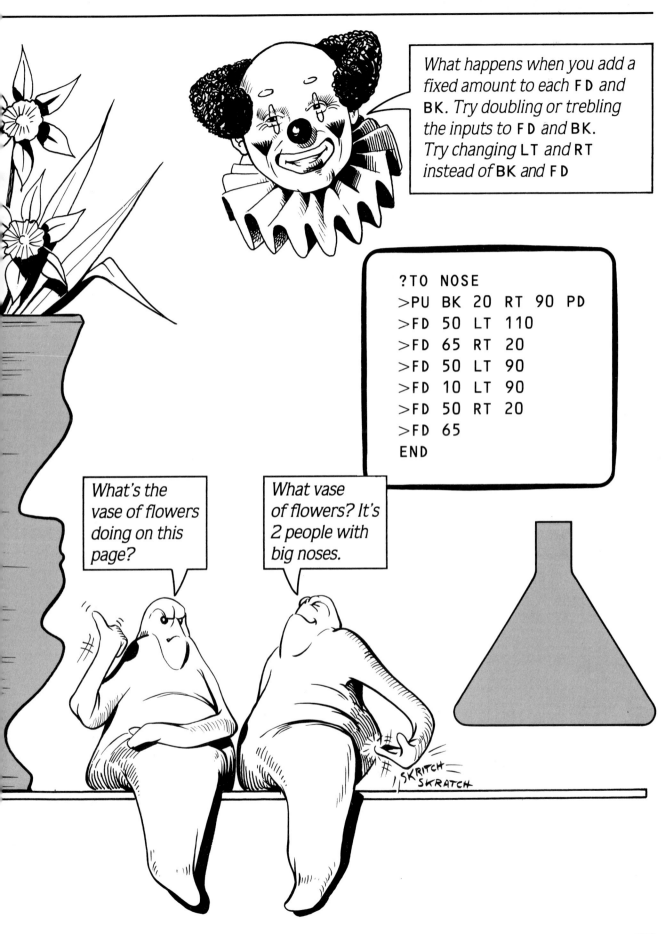

What happens when you add a fixed amount to each FD and BK. Try doubling or trebling the inputs to FD and BK. Try changing LT and RT instead of BK and FD

```
?TO NOSE
>PU BK 20 RT 90 PD
>FD 50 LT 110
>FD 65 RT 20
>FD 50 LT 90
>FD 10 LT 90
>FD 50 RT 20
>FD 65
END
```

What's the vase of flowers doing on this page?

What vase of flowers? It's 2 people with big noses.

SKRITCH SKRATCH

Breaking up

Sometimes a procedure gets so complicated that it is very hard to find the bug. You can often chop a procedure up into subprocedures. A tree can become two bits — a trunk and a top. You may have two problems instead of one, but each bit will probably be easier than the original problem. Try writing the subprocedures for TREE.

```
TO TRUNK          TO TREE          TO TOP
. . . . .         TRUNK            . . . . .
. . . . .         TOP              . . . . .
. . . . .         END              . . . . .
END                                END
```

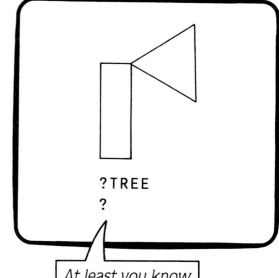

```
?TREE
?
```

At least you know where the bug is and which sub-procedure to edit.

I'm going to make a procedure
TO TOADSTOOL
BOTTOMBIT
TOPBIT
LEFTSPOT
RIGHTSPOT
END
I think.

I think I can do the spots okay. I'll start there and build round them.

Ogol has a plan. He knows what subprocedures he will need. He has worked out what order to do things in. He has even written a procedure — TOADSTOOL. Will it work yet?

Orcim has found part of the problem that looks easy — the spots. She's decided to do them and then make the subprocedure for the harder bits. Then she'll fit them together.

 Which way would you choose?

Subprocedures

Top level

```
TO SUBMARINE
HULL
PORTHOLES
TOWER
PERISCOPE
FLAG
END
```

Level 1

```
TO TOWER
BOTTOMBLOCK
MIDDLEBLOCK
TOPBLOCK
END
```

Level 2

```
TO MIDDLEBLOCK
REPEAT
2[FD 20 RT 90 FD 50 RT 90]
END
```

Super turtle

Super turtles specialize in patterns made like this:-

1. Define a procedure.
2. Define a second procedure which uses the first one.
3. Define a third procedure which uses the second one.
4. Define a fourth procedure which uses the third one.

And so on.

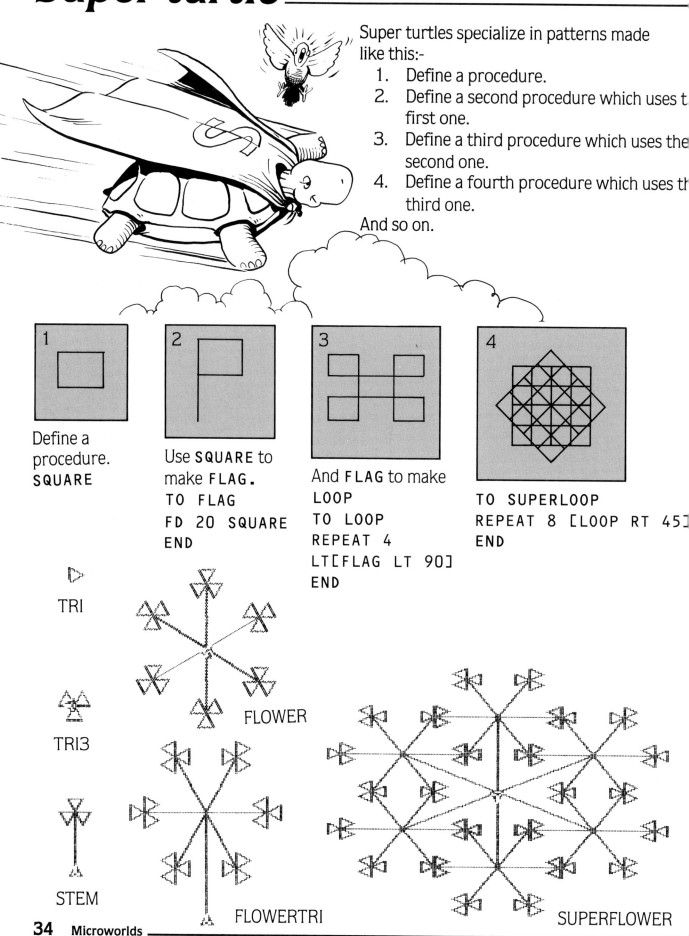

1

Define a procedure.
SQUARE

2

Use SQUARE to make FLAG.
TO FLAG
FD 20 SQUARE
END

3

And FLAG to make LOOP
TO LOOP
REPEAT 4
LT[FLAG LT 90]
END

4

TO SUPERLOOP
REPEAT 8 [LOOP RT 45]
END

TRI

TRI3

STEM

FLOWER

FLOWERTRI

SUPERFLOWER

Building blocks

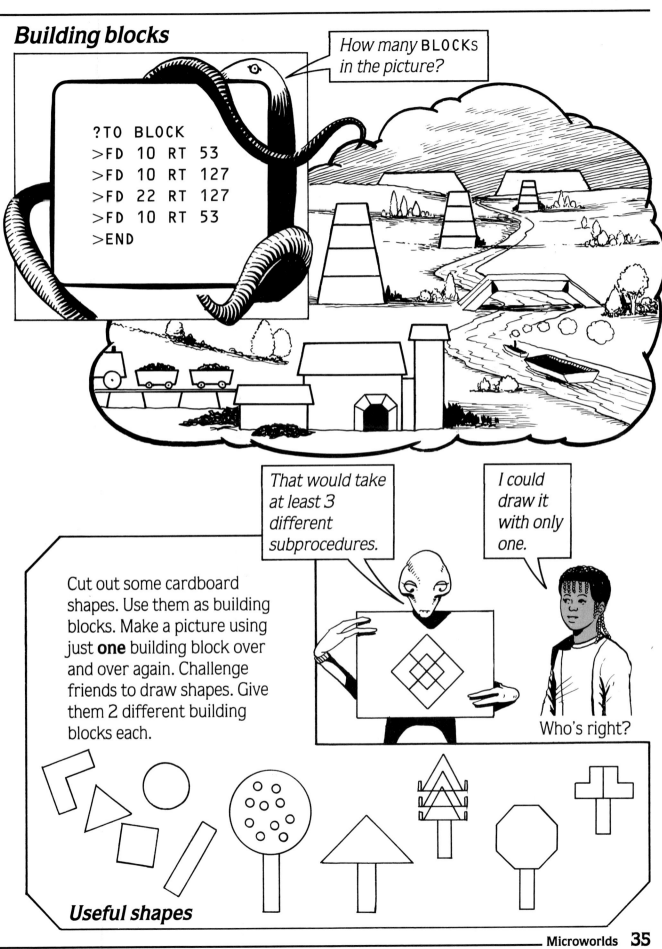

How many BLOCKS in the picture?

```
?TO BLOCK
>FD 10 RT 53
>FD 10 RT 127
>FD 22 RT 127
>FD 10 RT 53
>END
```

That would take at least 3 different subprocedures.

I could draw it with only one.

Who's right?

Cut out some cardboard shapes. Use them as building blocks. Make a picture using just **one** building block over and over again. Challenge friends to draw shapes. Give them 2 different building blocks each.

Useful shapes

Spider

Using the letters in the word SPIDER you can make lots more words...
PRIDES DRIPS PIES DRIES and so on.

Print 10 words from SPIDER on the screen. Jane wants to do the same thing with ARACHNIDAE.

Moving

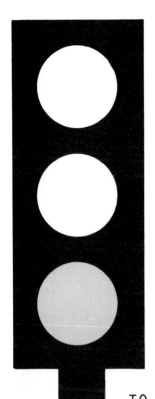

Making subprocedures to MOVE the turtle from one subprocedure to the next can help to make writing and debugging them easier. A MOVE subprocedure generally looks like this:

| PU | where to go | PD |

Where to go may involve instructions like FD and BK.

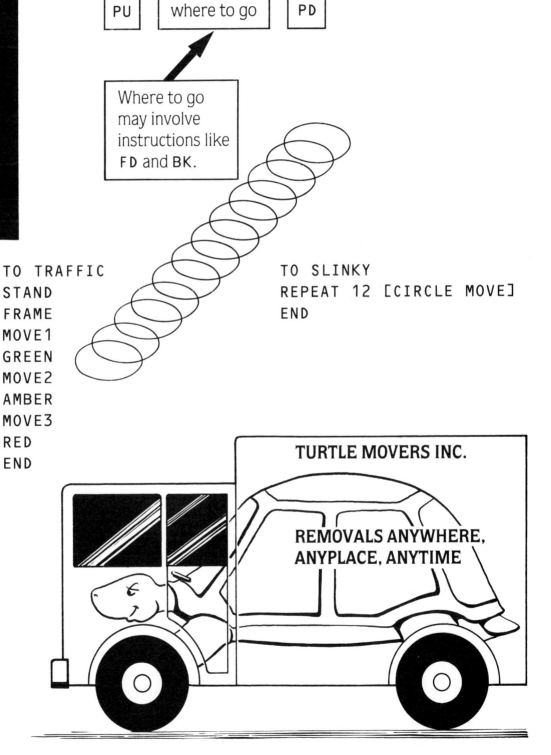

```
TO TRAFFIC
STAND
FRAME
MOVE1
GREEN
MOVE2
AMBER
MOVE3
RED
END
```

```
TO SLINKY
REPEAT 12 [CIRCLE MOVE]
END
```

TURTLE MOVERS INC.

REMOVALS ANYWHERE, ANYPLACE, ANYTIME

Try using MOVE to draw a truck.

Tiles

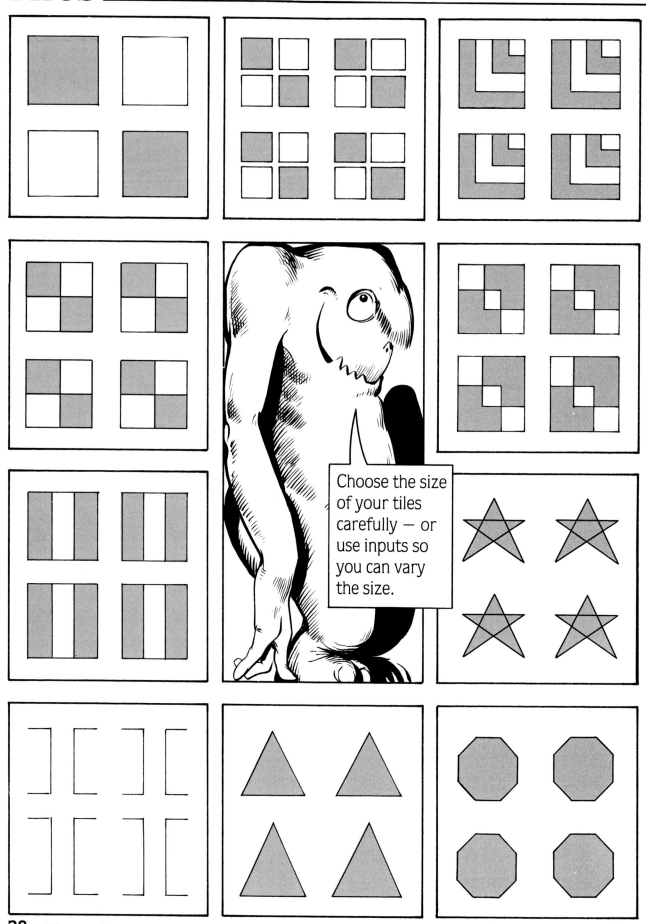

Choose the size of your tiles carefully — or use inputs so you can vary the size.

Jeff and Jane's computer screen is 280 turtle steps wide and 240 turtle steps down. (Yours may be different, it's worth checking.) 10 rows of 10 tiles, with gaps, fit nicely on the screen.

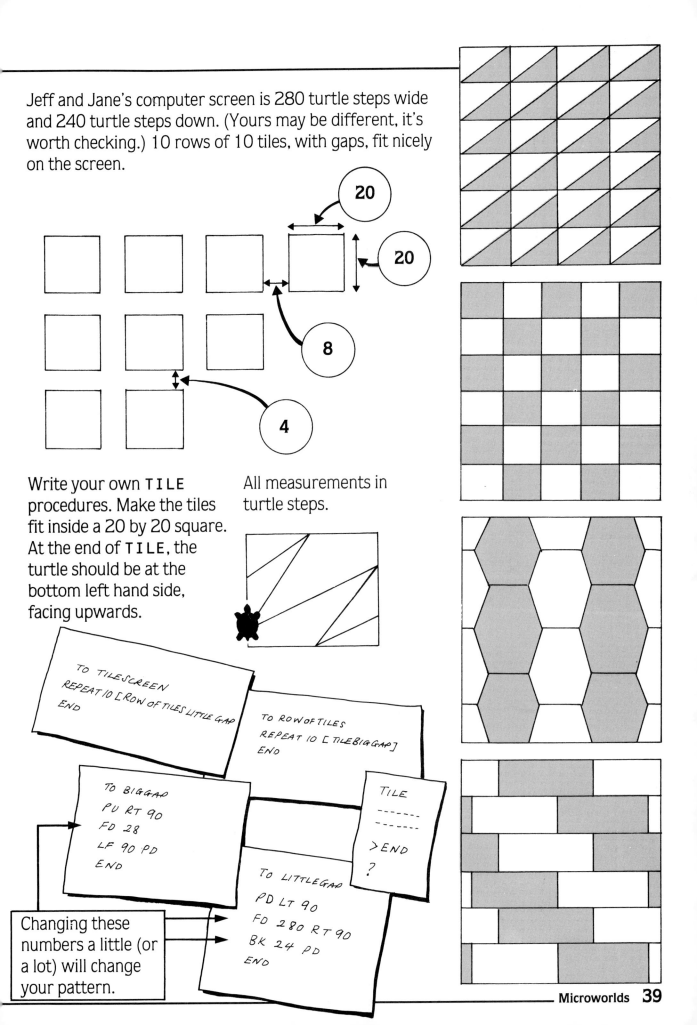

Write your own **TILE** procedures. Make the tiles fit inside a 20 by 20 square. At the end of **TILE**, the turtle should be at the bottom left hand side, facing upwards.

All measurements in turtle steps.

```
TO TILESCREEN
REPEAT 10 [ ROW OF TILES LITTLE GAP ]
END
```

```
TO ROW OF TILES
REPEAT 10 [ TILE BIG GAP ]
END
```

```
TO BIG GAP
PU RT 90
FD 28
LF 90 PD
END
```

```
TILE
- - - - - -
- - - - - -

> END
?
```

```
TO LITTLE GAP
PD LT 90
FD 280 RT 90
BK 24 PD
END
```

Changing these numbers a little (or a lot) will change your pattern.

Top down

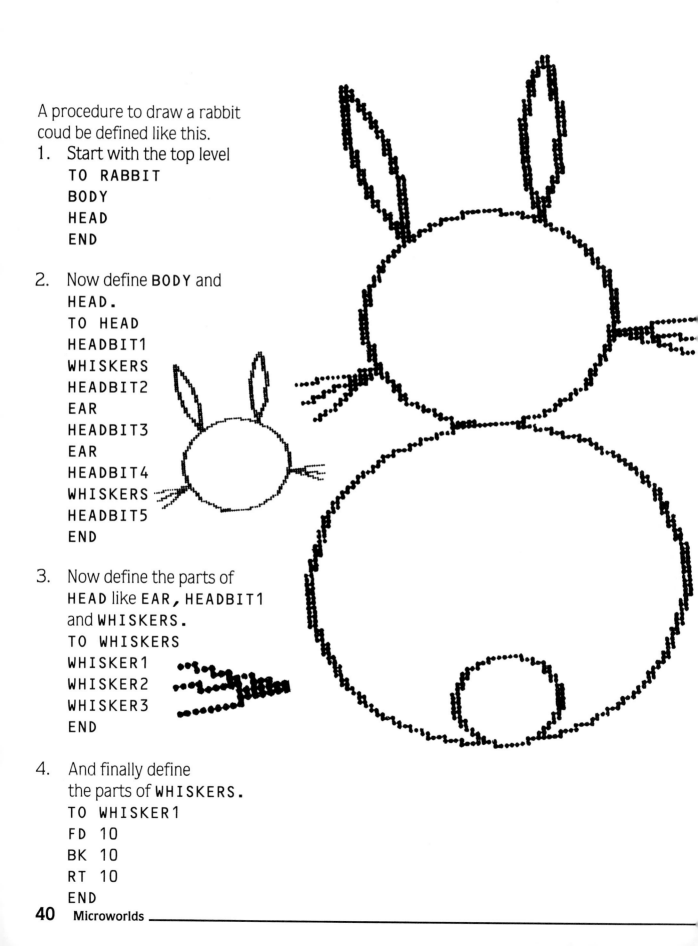

A procedure to draw a rabbit coud be defined like this.

1. Start with the top level

```
TO RABBIT
BODY
HEAD
END
```

2. Now define BODY and HEAD.

```
TO HEAD
HEADBIT1
WHISKERS
HEADBIT2
EAR
HEADBIT3
EAR
HEADBIT4
WHISKERS
HEADBIT5
END
```

3. Now define the parts of HEAD like EAR, HEADBIT1 and WHISKERS.

```
TO WHISKERS
WHISKER1
WHISKER2
WHISKER3
END
```

4. And finally define the parts of WHISKERS.

```
TO WHISKER1
FD 10
BK 10
RT 10
END
```

Bottom up

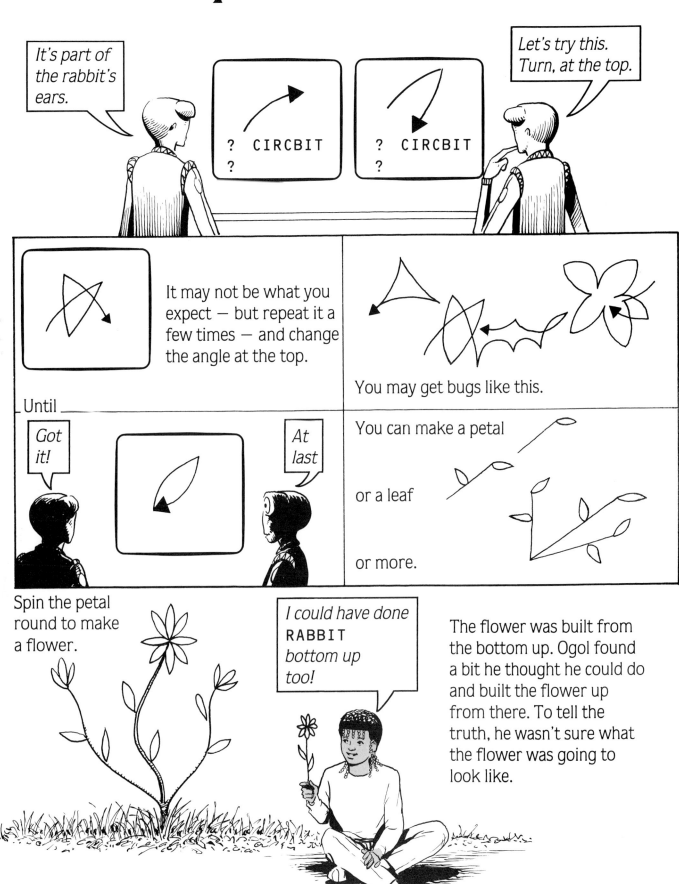

It's part of the rabbit's ears.

? CIRCBIT
?

? CIRCBIT
?

Let's try this. Turn, at the top.

It may not be what you expect — but repeat it a few times — and change the angle at the top.

You may get bugs like this.

Until

Got it!

At last

You can make a petal

or a leaf

or more.

Spin the petal round to make a flower.

I could have done RABBIT bottom up too!

The flower was built from the bottom up. Ogol found a bit he thought he could do and built the flower up from there. To tell the truth, he wasn't sure what the flower was going to look like.

Identikit

You can write your own identikit procedure — perhaps with a little help from your friends. Write the procedure for the whole face, then the subprocedures — or the other way round as Jeff and Jane did, whichever feels comfortable. You'll need **MOVE** subprocedures between the parts of the face.

We made lots of different versions of each part of the face.

CATEYE

SHUTEYE

DIAMONDEYE

TRINOSE   BOBBLE

TRNOSE   NOSE

Mouths

Face shapes

And then we wrote a procedure to put them together...

and swapped in different eyes and noses until we had something we wanted.

```
?TO CLOWN
>FACE
>MOUTH
>EYEL
>EYER
>NOSE
>HAIR
>END
```

You could start your face with the eyes. Here are a few to get you started.

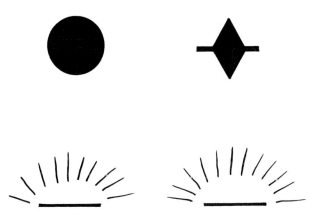

```
TO SHUTEYE
EYE
LASH
MOVE
EYE
LASH
END
```

```
TO LASH
REPEAT 20[PU FD 20 PD FD 5 BK 5 PU BK 20 RT 10]
END
```

(The direction of the turtle at the start of the lash matters!)

```
TO CATEYE
RT 90
HALFCIRCLE
RT 90
HALFCIRCLE
END
```

You could use your identikit program to make masks, birthday cards, whatever.

There's a bug somewhere.

Seen one, you've seen them all

TRIANGLE FOREST

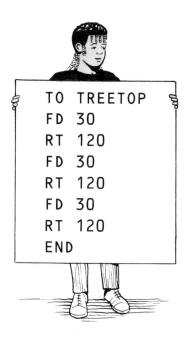

```
TO TREETOP
FD 30
RT 120
FD 30
RT 120
FD 30
RT 120
END
```

Jeff edited Jane's procedure for TREETOP. Try typing

TREETOP 50

TREETOP 73

TREETOP 0

↑

Don't forget the space.

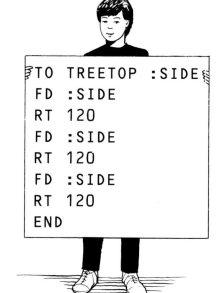

```
TO TREETOP :SIDE
FD :SIDE
RT 120
FD :SIDE
RT 120
FD :SIDE
RT 120
END
```

:SIDE is an INPUT to the procedure TREETOP.

You can have any size TREETOP you like; but how does it work? What happens if you type TREETOP on it's own? Try editing Jeff's procedure and using another word instead of SIDE (like TREETOP :OGOL) Try explaining how you think inputs work to a friend.

Each time you write a procedure the computer keeps it ready for you to call up.

Some procedures need INPUTS. You've been using them since you started LOGO.

FD, RT, SETPC all need inputs. Others don't, like PENUP. Make your own lists of procedures which do and don't need inputs.

There are two things you have to remember when you define a procedure with inputs.
1.   Don't forget the dots:
2.   Don't forget to **name** the input on the title line.

TO ☐   : ☐
     ↑   ↑
procedure name input name.

If you forget the dots, LOGO thinks your input is just another procedure.

What happens then? What if two procedures have the same name for their inputs?

Changing angles

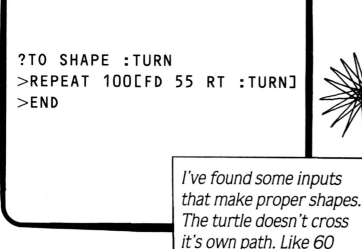

```
?TO SHAPE :TURN
>REPEAT 100[FD 55 RT :TURN]
>END
```

I've found some inputs that make proper shapes. The turtle doesn't cross it's own path. Like 60 and 30.
For some inputs the turtle crosses over itself. I like them better.

What does the input :TURN do?

Try   SHAPE 60
         SHAPE 30
         SHAPE 120

What input would make a square?
What input made this sponge?

Try   SHAPE 63
         SHAPE 58
         SHAPE 100

And I certainly don't need 100 REPEATs for a square.

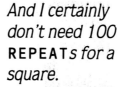

```
TO SHAPE :TURN
REPEAT 100[FD 40 RT :TURN]
END
```

How many REPEATs for a triangle?
For a pentagon or a hexagon look on the next page.

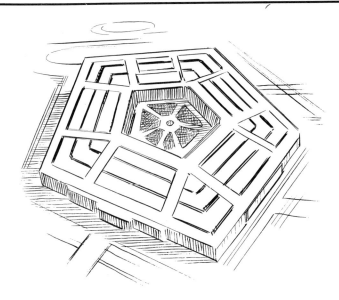

This building is in America. It is called the Pentagon because it has 5 sides. What input to SHAPE will draw a pentagon?

Honeycombs are made up of hexagon-shaped cells. Hexagons are shapes with 6 sides. Can you make a hexagon with SHAPE?

Shape challenge

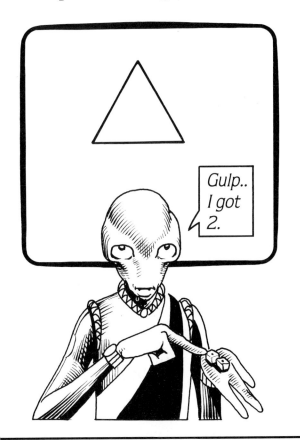

★ Take 2 dice and throw them.
★ Add up the numbers.
★ Find the input to SHAPE which will make a picture with that number of sides. (E.g. you throw a 3 and a 5. You need to find the input to SHAPE which gives an 8 sided shape.)

Skyscrapers

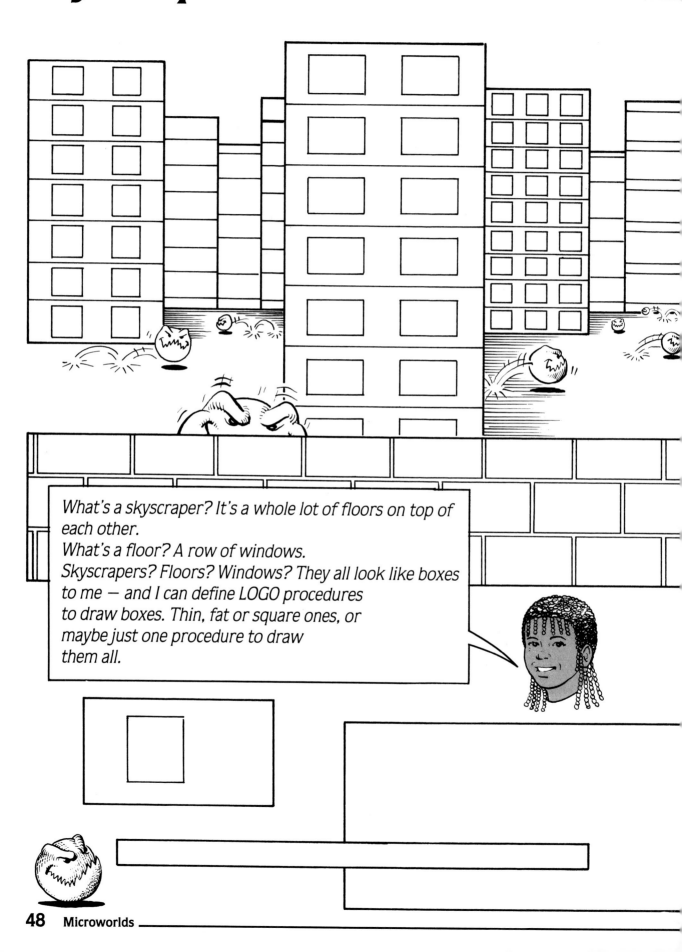

What's a skyscraper? It's a whole lot of floors on top of each other.
What's a floor? A row of windows.
Skyscrapers? Floors? Windows? They all look like boxes to me — and I can define LOGO procedures to draw boxes. Thin, fat or square ones, or maybe just one procedure to draw them all.

BOX has two inputs :WIDTH
and :HEIGHT. Here's one version
of BOX. Maybe you
could do it quicker using
REPEAT.

:WIDTH

:HEIGHT

```
?TO BOX :WIDTH :HEIGHT
>FD :HEIGHT RT 90
>FD :WIDTH RT 90
>FD :HEIGHT RT 90
>FD :WIDTH RT 90
>END
```

*Each pair of inputs
adds up to 100. I wonder
if that matters?*

Try

```
BOX 10 90
BOX 20 80
BOX 30 70
BOX 40 60
```

Use BOX **to build a** FLOOR.

THIRDMOVE

```
TO FLOOR
BOX 20 100
FIRSTMOVE
BOX 10 20
SECONDMOVE
BOX 10 20
THIRDMOVE
END
```

Then decide on the number of floors —
you could make the number of floors
an input to a procedure SKYSCRAPER.

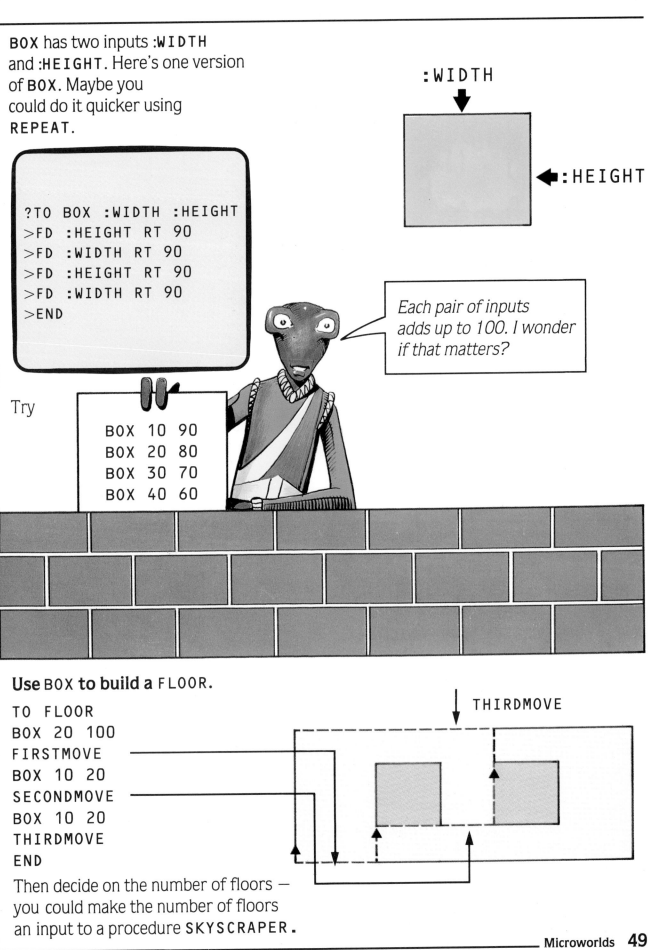

Windmills

Take a triangle.

Give it an input.

Put them together
in groups

and rotate them.

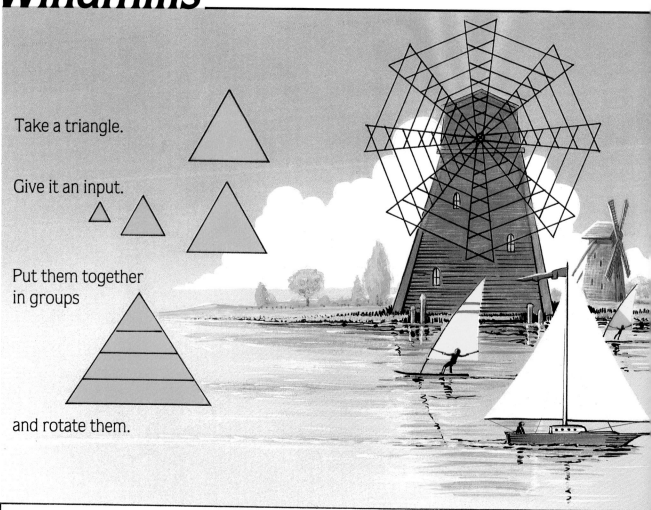

Inputs don't have to be about size. Take
a favourite procedure and make a
new procedure.

```
TO NEWBUTTERFLY :WHATCOLOUR
SETBG :WHATCOLOUR
BUTTERFLY
END
```

Then try
```
NEWBUTTERFLY 2
NEWBUTTERFLY 6
```

an so on. Try the same idea with SETPC or both.
SETBG is short for SETBACKGROUND colour.
SETPC is short for SETPENCOLOUR

BUTTERFLY

*But won't the background
and the pen be the same
colour? I wonder.*

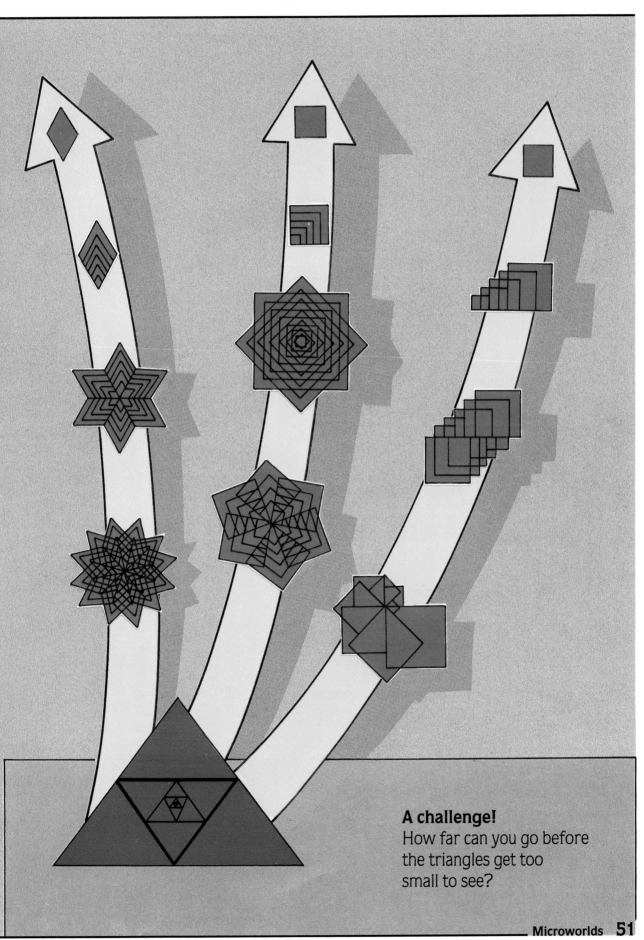

A challenge!
How far can you go before
the triangles get too
small to see?

Wherever next?

When you throw dice, the numbers which come up are random — they can be any number between one and six.

In the box below are six rows of numbers. One row is random. All the others have patterns if you can find them.

Using **PRINT RANDOM □**, *LOGO will give me random numbers. Will I ever get a 12 using* **PRINT RANDOM 12?**

```
?PRINT RANDOM 12
6
?PRINT RANDOM 12
2
?PRINT RANDOM 12
11
```

1	2	3	4	5	6	?
2	4	6	8	10	12	?
30	36	42	48	54	60	?
31	28	31	30	31	30	?
15	2	71	14	9	11	?
24	21	18	15	12	9	?

```
TO EXPLODE
REPEAT 100 [SETPC
RANDOM 6
RT RANDOM 360 [FD 100
BK 100]]
END
```
What happens to **EXPLODE** if you change this to **RANDOM 100?**

```
TO PAINTING
SETBG RANDOM 5
REPEAT 100
[SETPC RANDOM 6 FD
RANDOM 200 RIGHT 90]
END
```

You can make the turtle
walk RANDOM round the screen.

Use the LOGO command WRAP so
that you can see the turtle even if
it walks off the screen.

```
TO WALK
WRAP
REPEAT 1000[FD 10 RT RANDOM 360]
END
```

WRAP makes sure
that if the turtle
walks off one side
of the screen, it
appears on the
opposite side of the
screen.

This makes the
turtle turn a
random
amount.

```
?TO PICSHOW
>REPEAT 10 [WAIT 60
 SETBG RANDOM 6]
>END
?
```

You can make the amount the
turtle goes forward random
too. Try a walk and see if
you can make the turtle
cover most of the screen
as it walks around.

The WAIT command freezes the action
for a little while.
    WAIT 60—the computer waits one second
    WAIT 3600—the computer waits one minute
Use WAIT with the WALK routine
(add WAIT 200 and SETPCRANDOM 7]
and produce a spectacular show.
Find out how many pen colours there are on
your system.

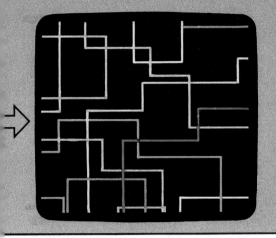

Hunt the spook

TO POPUP
HIDETURTLE
PD
SPOOK
PE
SPOOK
PD
SHOWTURTLE
END

TO SPOOK
FD 20
RT 54
FD 13
RT 78
FD 13
RT 51
FD 20
RT 30
FD 8
RT 120
FD 8
LT 120
FD 8
RT 120
FD 8
RT 30
LT 90
PD 4
RT 90
END

Some people believe there's a ghost haunting this castle.

A ghost. What does it look like?

Well, sort of wispy and pale.

I could write a procedure to make the spook pop up in all sorts of different places, using RANDOM.

Since ancient times, patterns made up of triangles have been used to decorate floors, walls, rugs and clothing.

To make triangular patterns, I need to colour in the triangles. My idea is to draw triangles really close together.

Some versions of LOGO have a `FILL` command to colour in shapes like the turtle on the right. Try it out to make shapes like these, or try Jane's idea.

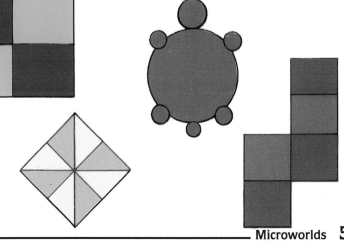

How does your garden grow?

What angle do
you need to
make a petal?
How big is `SIZE`?

```
?TO PETAL :SIZE
>HALFPETAL :SIZE
>RIGHT  ?
>HALFPETAL :SIZE
>END
```

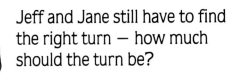

```
?TO TOP
>REPEAT 6[PETAL RIGHT  ? ]
>END
```

*Oh no — a bug —
`PETAL` needs
an input.*

```
?TO TOP :SIZE
>REPEAT 6[PETAL
:SIZE RT  ? ]
>END
```

Jeff and Jane still have to find
the right turn — how much
should the turn be?

Now for `STEM`. Jeff tried out `STEM` with
the same input as `TOP`.

```
TO STEM :SIZE
BACK :SIZE
END
```

`STEM 3` with `TOP 3` made a fine flower
but a short stem. `STEM 30` with `TOP 30`
gave an enormous flower. Can you solve
the bug? Here's a clue. The final procedure
looks like

```
TO FLOWER :SIZE
TOP :SIZE
STEM :SIZE* □
END
```

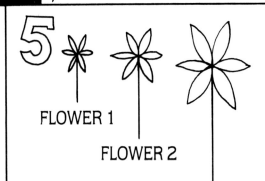

FLOWER 1

FLOWER 2

FLOWER 3

Now you can vary the size
of your flowers.
How about varying the
number of petals — or the
colour or...?

Hills and forests

Doesn't look much like a hill to me.

Try lots of mountains — REPEAT 100[HILL 50] maybe.

```
TO HILL :SIZE
FD :SIZE
RT 120
FD :SIZE
LT 120
END
```

LOGO EDITOR

I think I can make it better.

If we went forward a RANDOM amount each time, the hills would be different sizes.

Procedures by [Alex Anders Andrew Anne
Ben Catherine Chris David Dawn Debbie
Frances Joanna Jonathon Kathryn Kerry G.
Kerry M. Leighton Matthew Michelle Nicholas
Paul Rachel Robert Rosemary Ruth
Sarah Ed. Sarah El. Steven Tony]
From *Turtleland*, AUCBE.

Over & Over & Over & Over

Beat the clock

**Lay low leather
Fair flung feather
Wheat when worms
Gotta get germs**

The challenge is to read the poem fast for a minute without laughing.

You need two or more people.
1. The first person reads the poem. When they finish they start again.
2. The second person does the same but begins when the first person gets to

   the end of the first line.
3. And so on for all the players.

If you set up two mirrors facing each other the reflections go on for ever.

```
?TO GOSSIP
>PRINT "HELLO
>PRINT "GOODBYE
>GOSSIP
>END
```

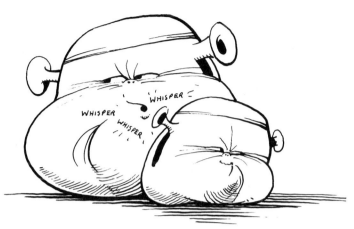

These recursive procedures go on for ever. You can stop them by pressing special keys (or key). On Jane and Jeff's computer, it's CTRL and G together. Other ways of stopping over and over procedures in the procedures themselves are suggested on page 72.

What does it do, Ogol?

```
?TO TWIST
>SQUARE
>RT 43
>TWIST
>END
```

It draws a square, and then the turtle turns right a bit and draws another square. That's all I think.

Is Ogol right? What do you think TWIST draws? Make a guess and then check it on the computer.

Look no hands!

The autopilot in our spaceship allows you to enter the co-ordinates of the place you want to go to and then just takes you there.

This is position [31 24] It's 31 along from the centre of the screen and 24 up.

The centre of the screen is position [0 0]

There's a sort of turtle autopilot command called SETPOS You tell the turtle the position of the place you want to go to and the turtle goes straight there.

Start with a clearscreen and try out

```
?SETPOS [1 10]
?SETPOS [50 3]
?SETPOS [8 100]
```

Suppose you get lost?

```
?TO PUZZLE
>HT
>FD 10 RT 21
>FD 17 LT 10
>FD 20
>END
```

Then you can find out where you are with POS. What position do you think the turtle is at now? Try typing PRINT POS Orcim.

Try

```
TO GALAXY
REPEAT 100 [PU SETX RANDOM 200 SETY RANDOM 200 PD DOT]
END
```

SETX AND SETY
SETX tells the turtle how far to go along.
SETY tells the turtle how far to go up.

Some computers have DOT built in. If yours doesn't, it's easy to write.
```
TO DOT
FD 1 BK 1
END
```
Why not edit it to make the stars different colours?

Mission No. 117724843373B
Please park 8 weather satellites
around galaxy. Park them where
you like as long as there is at
least one in each quarter
of the galaxy. Satellites
must be at least 20 grentons
apart or their gravity fields
may interfere with each other.
Message ends.

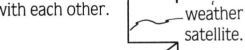
A Mark 1
weather
satellite.

Intergalactic Printer

Carry out the mission using the
LOGO screen as a map of the
galaxy. On the map,
1 turtle step is one
grenton.

Surprise, surprise

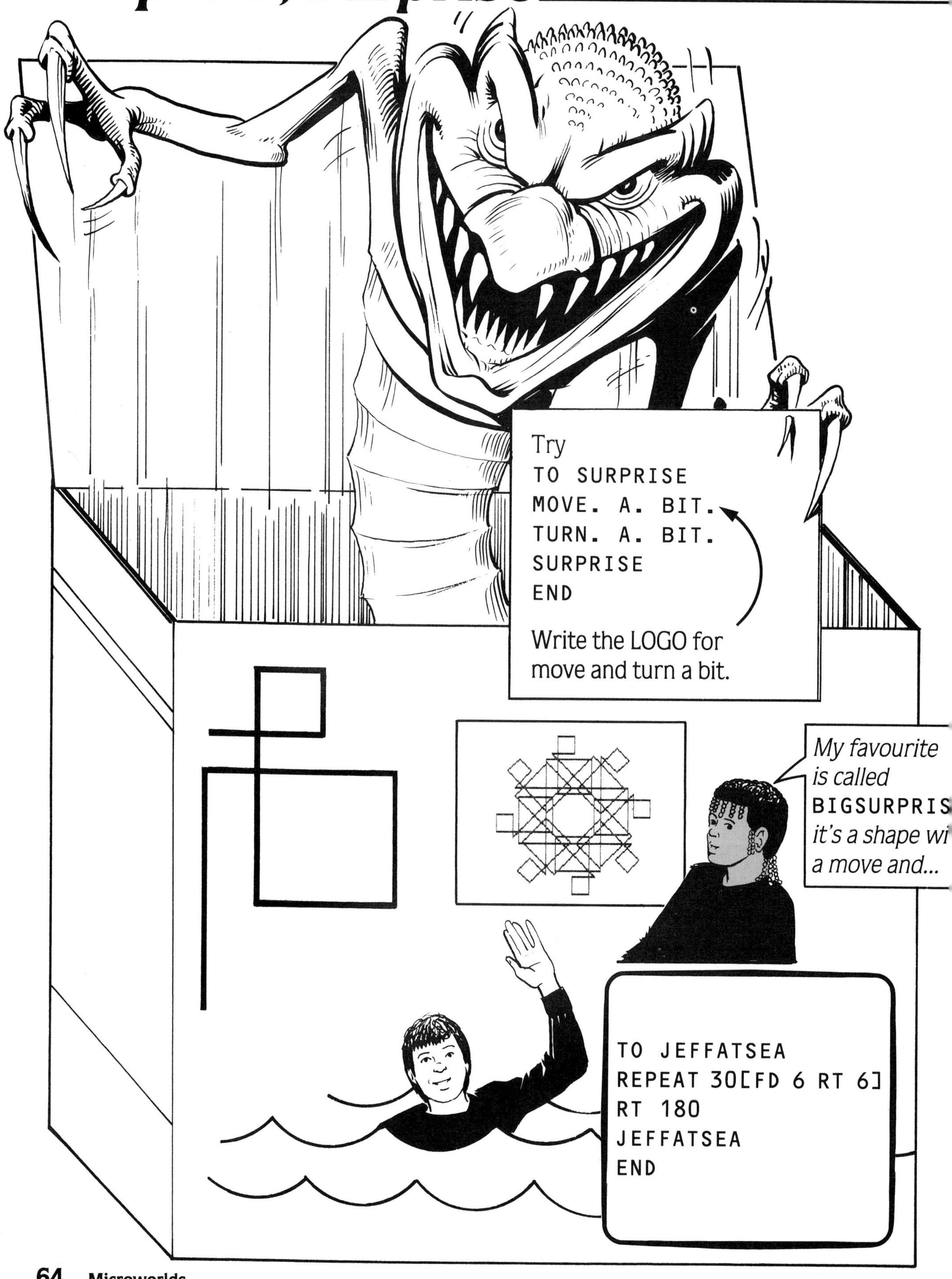

Try

```
TO SURPRISE
MOVE. A. BIT.
TURN. A. BIT.
SURPRISE
END
```

Write the LOGO for
move and turn a bit.

*My favourite
is called
BIGSURPRIS
it's a shape wi
a move and...*

```
TO JEFFATSEA
REPEAT 30[FD 6 RT 6]
RT 180
JEFFATSEA
END
```

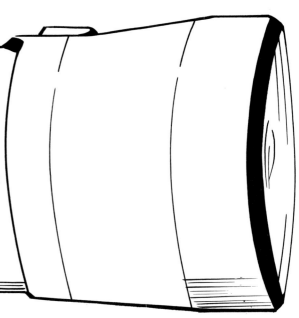

SETSCRUNCH is a LOGO word for squashing your LOGO pictures. Borrow a torch. Wait until it is dark and switch off all the lights. Point the torch straight at a wall and switch it on. Tilt it to get a circle of light. Now tilt the torch gradually up towards the ceiling. As it moves, the shape of the patch of light changes — the sort of change **SETSCRUNCH** makes to LOGO shapes.

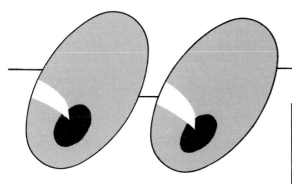

SETSCRUNCH *will turn my circle into an oval.*

```
?CLEARSCREEN
?SETSCRUNCH 2
?CIRCLE
```

SETSCRUNCH needs a number as an input. Try some really big and very small numbers. If **SETSCRUNCH** doesn't work on your computer try **.SETSCR** or **.ASPECT** or look it up in the manual.

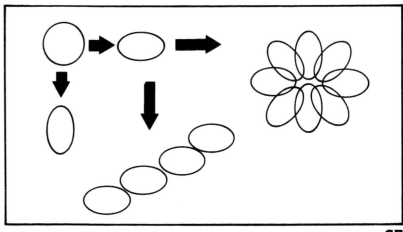

Creeping and walking

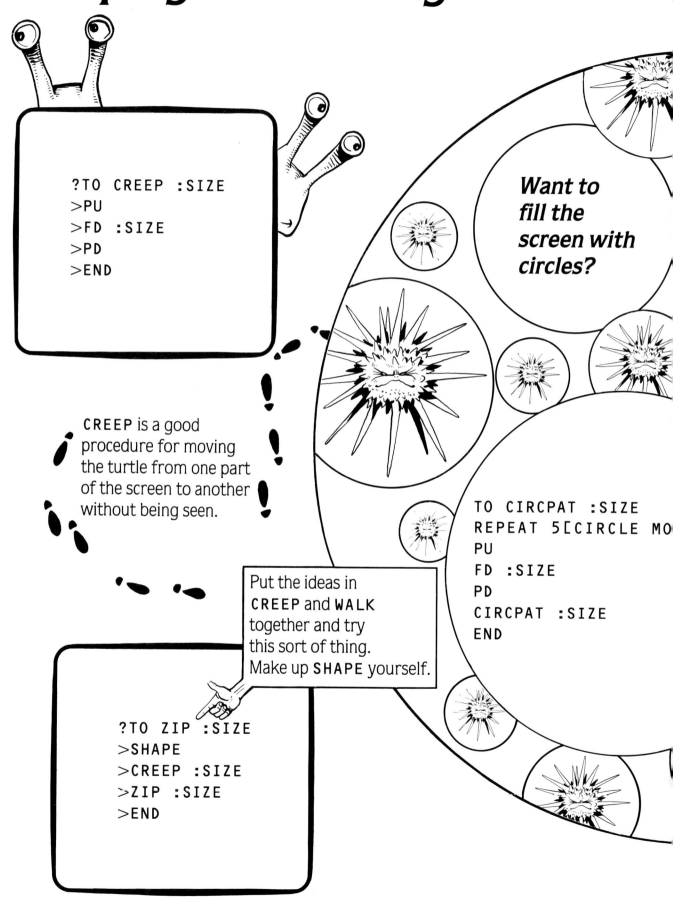

```
?TO CREEP :SIZE
>PU
>FD :SIZE
>PD
>END
```

CREEP is a good procedure for moving the turtle from one part of the screen to another without being seen.

Want to fill the screen with circles?

```
TO CIRCPAT :SIZE
REPEAT 5[CIRCLE MO
PU
FD :SIZE
PD
CIRCPAT :SIZE
END
```

Put the ideas in **CREEP** and **WALK** together and try this sort of thing. Make up **SHAPE** yourself.

```
?TO ZIP :SIZE
>SHAPE
>CREEP :SIZE
>ZIP :SIZE
>END
```

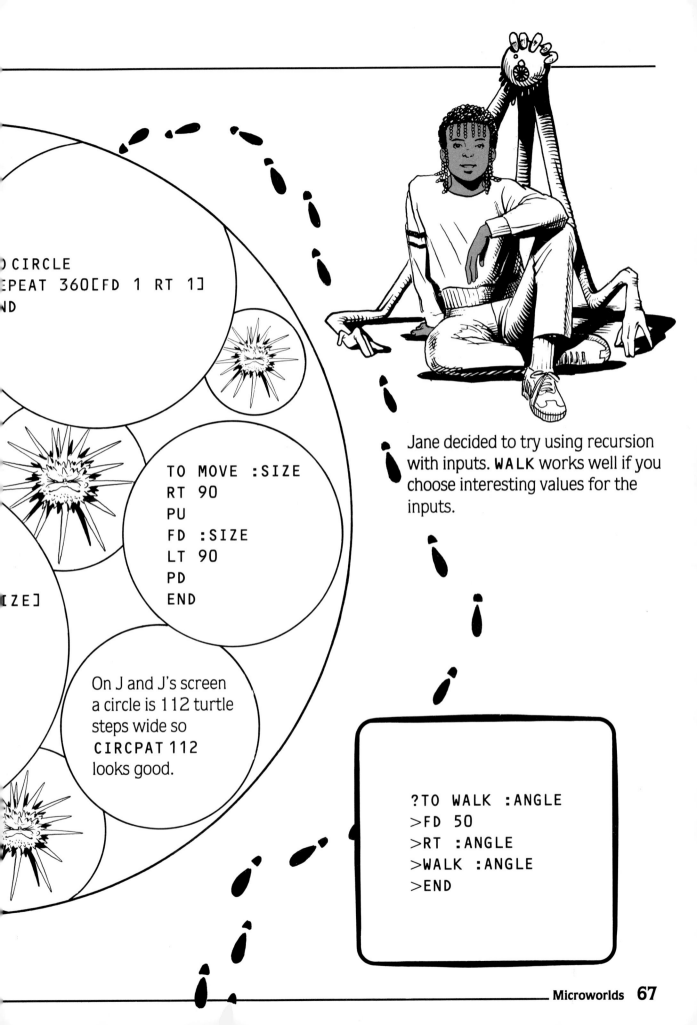

```
CIRCLE
REPEAT 360[FD 1 RT 1]
END
```

```
TO MOVE :SIZE
RT 90
PU
FD :SIZE
LT 90
PD
END
```

On J and J's screen
a circle is 112 turtle
steps wide so
`CIRCPAT` 112
looks good.

Jane decided to try using recursion
with inputs. **WALK** works well if you
choose interesting values for the
inputs.

```
?TO WALK :ANGLE
>FD 50
>RT :ANGLE
>WALK :ANGLE
>END
```

Let's get moving

In LOGO you can make a seagull's wings flap by drawing and erasing them. It looks best if you HIDETURTLE first.

```
?TO SEAGULL
>WINGS
>RT 180
>WINGS
>RT 180
>SEAGULL
>END
```

```
TO WINGS
RT 30
FD 10 BK 10
LT 60
FD 10 BK 10
PENERASE
FD 10 BK 10
RT 60
FD 10 BK 10
PENDOWN
LT 30
END
```

With the same trick you can get a matchstick figure to dance — a bit like Ogol doing Keep Fit.

Turtle escape

Jane's program is supposed to trap the turtle in a cage. Try it out and see if the turtle escapes.

```
TO TURTLETRAP
PD
REPEAT 4[FD 100 RT 90]
PU
SETPOS [5 5]
TRY
END
```

TURTLE TRAP
UNFAIR TO
TURTLES

```
TO TRY
PENUP
FD 5
RT 5
IF XCOR >95[RT 180]
IF XCOR <5[RT 180]
IF YCOR >95[RT 180]
IF YCOR <5[RT 180]
TRY
END
```

Rocket take off

```
TO ROCKET :SIZE
FD :SIZE
RT 45
FD :SIZE/4
RT 90
FD :SIZE/4
RT 45
FD :SIZE
RT 90
FD :SIZE*35/100
RT 90
END
```

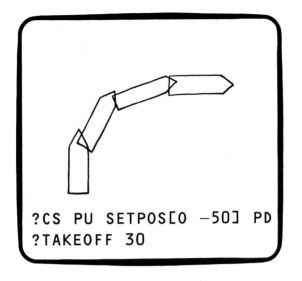

```
?CS PU SETPOS[0 −50] PD
?TAKEOFF 30
```

Can you find the `:ANGLE` so that the rocket blasts off and disappears at the top of the screen?

Drive the turtle

These LOGO procedures allow you to drive the turtle round the screen. To make the turtle turn to the left, press **L** and to make it turn to the right press **R**. Drive carefully and try not to let the turtle go off the edges of the screen.

```
TO TAKEOFF :ANGLE
ROCKET 50
PU FD 20 RT :ANGLE
PD
TAKEOFF :ANGLE
END
```

```
TO DRIVE
FORWARD 5
COMMAND
DRIVE
END

TO COMMAND
MAKE "COM READCHAR
IF :COM = "R [RIGHT 30]
IF :COM = "L [LEFT 30]
END
```

Polyspirals

```
?TO POLYSP :SIZE
>FD :SIZE
>RT 62
>POLYSP :SIZE+1
>END
```

I got all these by changing the 62 to different numbers.

And I got all these by changing the +1 as well

In all these polyspirals the turtle goes on forever. Can you work out how to make the turtle stop?

Inspirals

I've re-written `POLYSP` so the angle gets changed each time.

? INSPI 7

```
TO INSPI :ANGLE
FD 10
RIGHT :ANGLE
INSPI :ANGLE+1
END
```

Change `INSPI` in the same ways you changed `POLYSP`. Change the size of `FD` from 10 to something larger or smaller. Does `ANGLE` have to change by 1 each time?

Going dotty

Turtles can leave a dotty trail instead of the usual smooth one.

```
TO DOTTYWALK :DISTANCE
PENUP
FD :DISTANCE
PENDOWN
FD 1
BK 1
PENUP
RT 49
DOTTYWALK :DISTANCE+3
END
```

These are the LOGO commands which leave a dot sized trail.

These pictures are made by leaving a dot just before I change direction.

If only

If I steal lots of jewels I can retire to the Costa del Crime!

Recursion doesn't have to make procedures go on for ever. The computer will stop doing a procedure if it gets the LOGO command STOP. Normally you only want the procedure to stop if something special has happened like the turtle is facing in a particular direction.

THEY'D

STOP

!

I can use HEADING to stop my procedure

```
?TO BOX
>FD 50
>RT 90
>BOX
>END
```

Ogol and Orcim have taught Jane a K64 game using the LOGO command SETHEADING.
Player 1 keys
`CS HT SETHEADING RANDOM 360`
Player 2 guesses the way the turtle points. Use PRINT HEADING to check if player 2 is right.

Add the command
`IF HEADING = 0 [STOP]`
in the right place and it'll stop BOX. Experiment to find the right place.

The LOGO command I F can have a lot of different forms. They all have the same basic shape.

IF | Thing you want to be true | [List of things you want to happen if it is true]

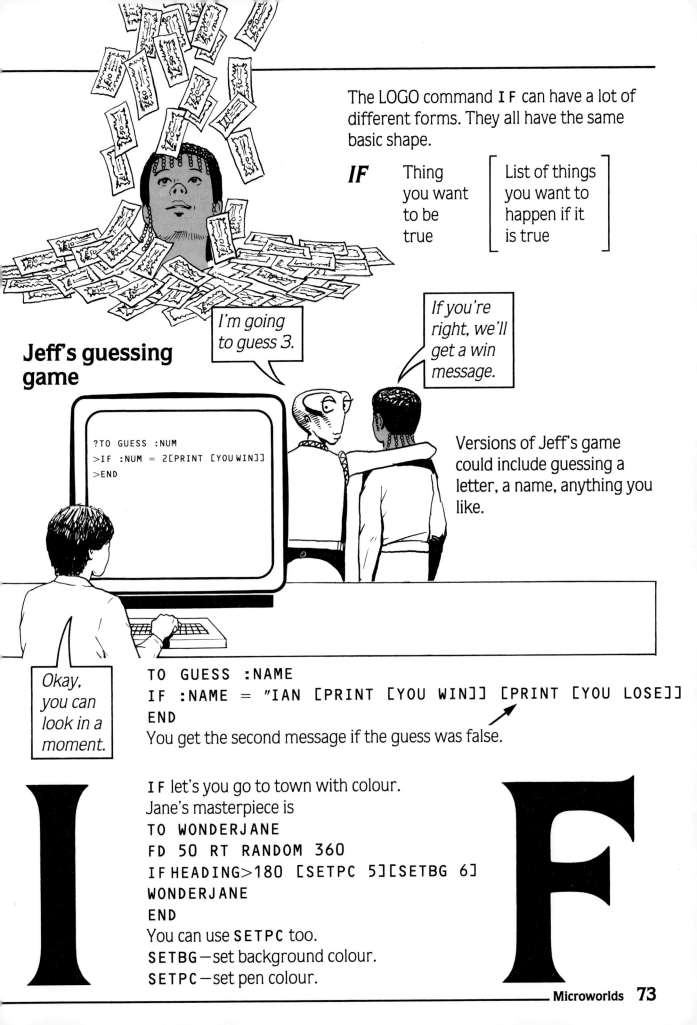

I'm going to guess 3.

If you're right, we'll get a win message.

Jeff's guessing game

```
?TO GUESS :NUM
>IF :NUM = 2[PRINT [YOU WIN]]
>END
```

Versions of Jeff's game could include guessing a letter, a name, anything you like.

Okay, you can look in a moment.

```
TO GUESS :NAME
IF :NAME = "IAN [PRINT [YOU WIN]] [PRINT [YOU LOSE]]
END
```
You get the second message if the guess was false.

I F let's you go to town with colour.
Jane's masterpiece is
```
TO WONDERJANE
FD 50 RT RANDOM 360
IF HEADING>180 [SETPC 5][SETBG 6]
WONDERJANE
END
```
You can use SETPC too.
SETBG—set background colour.
SETPC—set pen colour.

Counting down

```
?TO SHRINK :SIZE
>IF :SIZE <5[STOP]
>REPEAT 4 [FD :SIZE RT 90]
>PU
>FD 5 RT 90 FD 5 LT 90
>PD
>SHRINK :SIZE – 10
>END
?
```

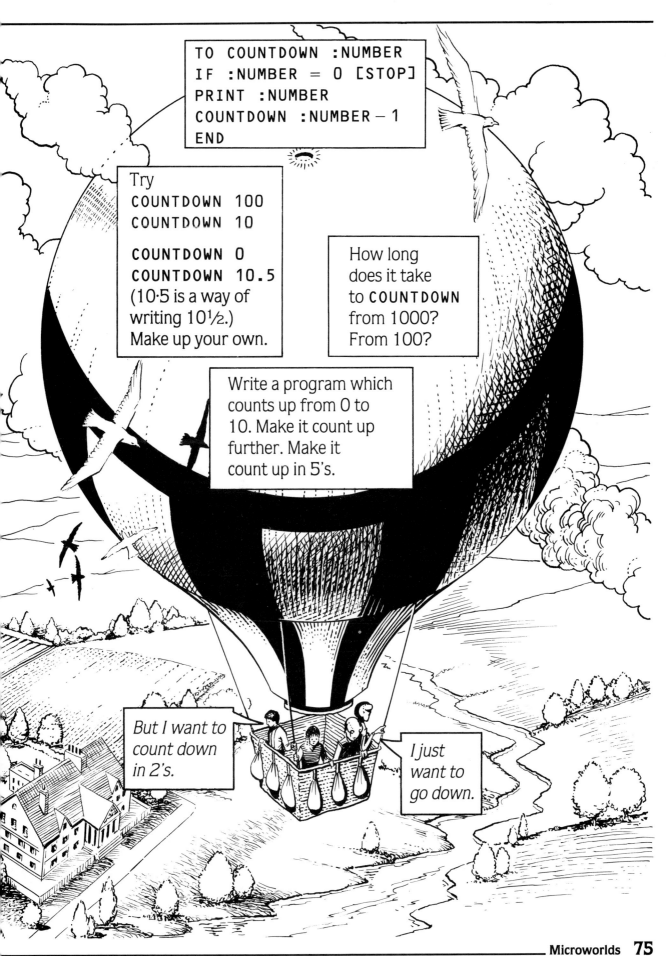

```
TO COUNTDOWN :NUMBER
IF :NUMBER = 0 [STOP]
PRINT :NUMBER
COUNTDOWN :NUMBER - 1
END
```

Try
COUNTDOWN 100
COUNTDOWN 10

COUNTDOWN 0
COUNTDOWN 10.5
(10·5 is a way of
writing 10½.)
Make up your own.

How long
does it take
to COUNTDOWN
from 1000?
From 100?

Write a program which
counts up from 0 to
10. Make it count up
further. Make it
count up in 5's.

But I want to count down in 2's.

I just want to go down.

Growing things

You can make filled shapes by growing them. Write a procedure TO SQUARE :SIZE and try out

    SQUARE 1
    SQUARE 2
    SQUARE 3 and so on, up to SQUARE 10.

Use your SQUARE procedure in

```
TO FILLSQUARE :SIZE
IF :SIZE >100 [STOP]
SQUARE :SIZE
FILLSQUARE :SIZE+1
END
```

All being well, you'll get a filled in square. How long is each side?

Can you get squares in red, green and blue by changing FILLSQUARE a little?

Curves which wiggle so much that they fill an area of space are called space filling curves.
Try a little editing on FILLSPACE to change the effect.

Try
START
FILLSPACE 256
and see what happens.

```
?TO START
>PU
>SETPOS [−100 −60]
>PD
>RT 90
>END
```

```
TO FILLSPACE :SIZE
IF :SIZE <4 [FD :SIZE STOP]
FILLSPACE :SIZE/2
LT 90
FILLSPACE :SIZE/2
RT 180
FILLSPACE :SIZE/2
LT 90
FILLSPACE :SIZE/2
END
```

Then I'm going to change the 4 in this IF line to 16 then 32 then 64 then 256 then..

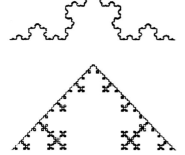

```
TO GROW :YEAR
BODY :YEAR      ←
FD :YEAR
RT 50
GROW :YEAR+1
END
```

This gives the shell a year's growth.
Then we get ready to grow a newshell at the end of the old one.

This gives next year's growth.

Many animals grow spiral shells. A new bit of shell grows each year.

So each of these rings means one year's growth.

Yes. They're called annual rings. This tree was 35 years old.

Can you write a LOGO procedure to grow circles like the annual rings?

Using
```
TO BODY :SIZE
REPEAT 2 [FD :SIZE LT 90 FD :SIZE/4 LT 90]
END
```

Try
```
GROW 0
```
Can you make bendy body sections more like a shell?

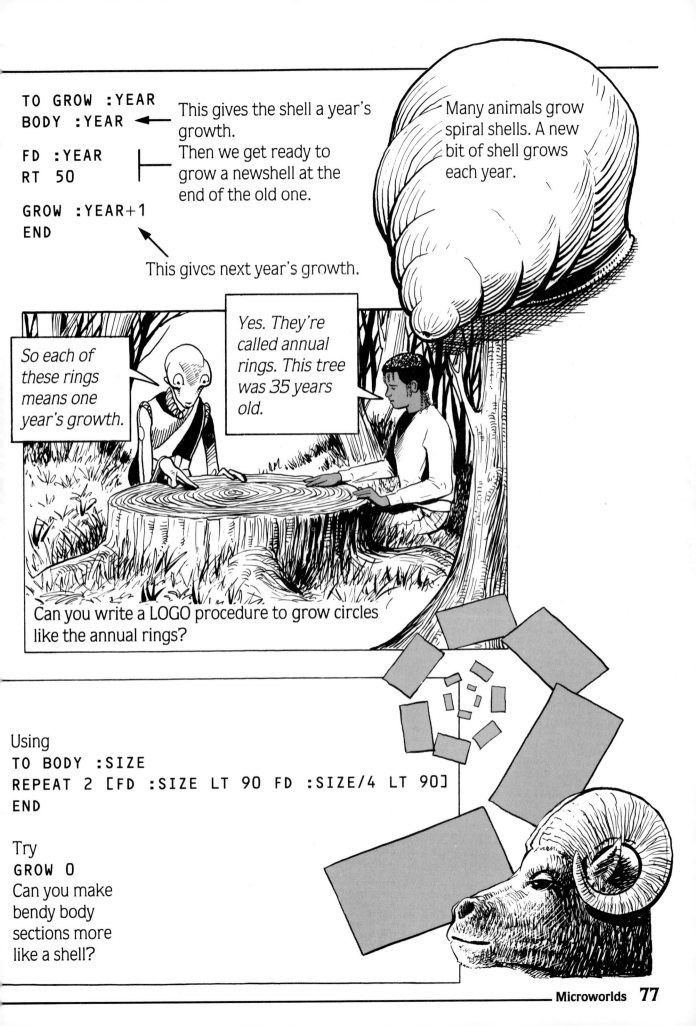

In perspective

Have you ever noticed how things look smaller as they get further away? This illusion is called perspective.

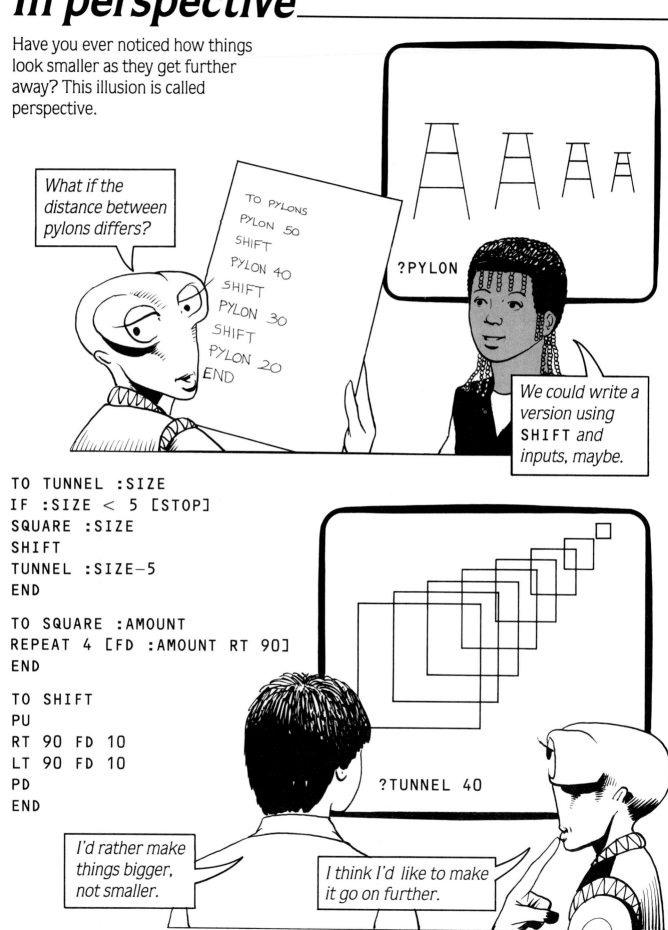

What if the distance between pylons differs?

```
TO PYLONS
PYLON 50
SHIFT
PYLON 40
SHIFT
PYLON 30
SHIFT
PYLON 20
END
```

?PYLON

We could write a version using SHIFT and inputs, maybe.

```
TO TUNNEL :SIZE
IF :SIZE < 5 [STOP]
SQUARE :SIZE
SHIFT
TUNNEL :SIZE−5
END

TO SQUARE :AMOUNT
REPEAT 4 [FD :AMOUNT RT 90]
END

TO SHIFT
PU
RT 90 FD 10
LT 90 FD 10
PD
END
```

?TUNNEL 40

I'd rather make things bigger, not smaller.

I think I'd like to make it go on further.

It would be
nice if each
lorry was a
different colour.

```
TO CLIMBHILL
LORRY 30 MOVE 30
LORRY 25 MOVE 25
LORRY 20 MOVE 20
LORRY 15 MOVE 15
LORRY 10 MOVE 10
END
```

Fruit machine

I helped too.

Orcim discovered fruit machines. We couldn't get her off them until Jane and I got one going in LOGO. Just as well, she was running out of money!

Here are some of the procedures. You'll have to write SQUARE, RECTANGLE and DIAMOND yourself.

```
TO FRUITMACHINE
CS
SHAPE RANDOM 3
END
```

```
TO SHAPE :CHOICE1
PU LT 90 FD 50 RT 90 PD
IF :CHOICE1 = 0[RECTANGLE]
IF :CHOICE1 = 1[SQUARE]
IF :CHOICE1 = 2[DIAMOND]
PU RT 90 FD 100 LT 90 PD
PRINT [PRESS THE SPACE BAR]
TWIZZLE READCHAR
END
```

Thanks, but I'm going to add more shapes and colour and and ....

```
TO TWIZZLE :STARTKEY
RECTANGLE PE RECTANGLE PD
SQUARE PE SQUARE PD
DIAMOND PE DIAMOND PD
SELECT RANDOM 3
END
```

```
TO SELECT :CHOICE2
IF CHOICE2 = 0[RECTANGLE]
IF CHOICE2 = 1[SQUARE]
IF CHOICE2 = 2[DIAMOND]
IF CHOICE2 = :CHOICE1[PRINT
[YOU WIN]] [PRINT[YOU LOSE]]
END
```

Yes Ogol just do it

Spdwrtng

My dds rprtr nd wrts fnny shrthnd mssgs lk ths. ts clldd spdwrtng. Hrs prcdr t chng nrml wrtng nt spdwrtng.

```
?TO SPEEDWRITING
>EX READCHAR
>SPEEDWRITING
>END
```

Mssgs n spdwrtng r lk mssgs n cd. Mk p n sy cd nd wrt prcdr t chng wrds typd nt th cd.

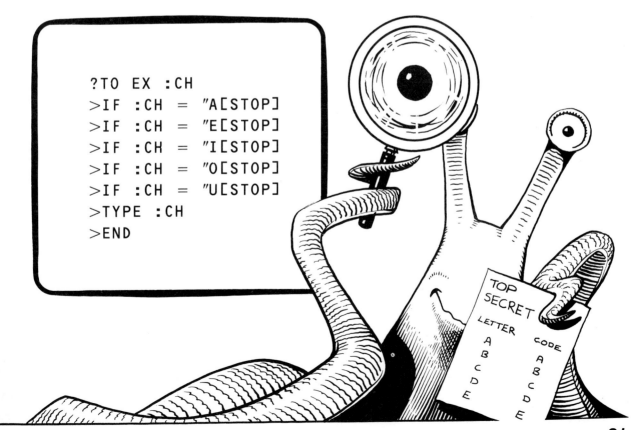

```
?TO EX :CH
>IF :CH = "A[STOP]
>IF :CH = "E[STOP]
>IF :CH = "I[STOP]
>IF :CH = "O[STOP]
>IF :CH = "U[STOP]
>TYPE :CH
>END
```

Sawing in half

It's safer to cut up LOGO shapes than aliens. Draw a shape on the screen, then move the turtle so it cuts the shape in half. Sounds easy? Try it.

Easy

Still easy

Half of something is not always obvious. Try these.

Gulp! Impossible.

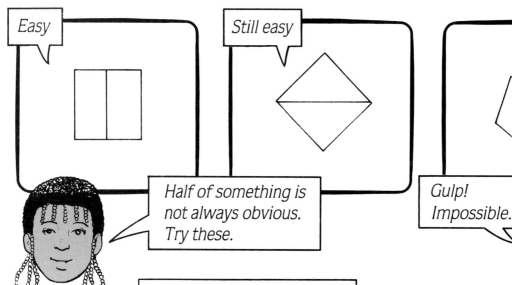

```
START
SAWNHALF 150
and
START
TRIHALF 150
and
START
SQHALF 150
```

Start
```
TO START
PU SETPOS [-100 -50] PD
END
```

Sawnhalf
```
TO SAWNHALF :SIZE
REPEAT 4 [FD :SIZE RT 90]
SAWNHALF :SIZE/1.41
END
```

Sqhalf
```
TO SQHALF :SIZE
REPEAT 4 [FD :SIZE RT 90]
RT 45
FD 1.41*:SIZE BK 0.71*:SIZE
RT 45
SQHALF :SIZE/2
END
```

Trihalf
```
TO TRIHALF :SIZE
REPEAT 3 [FD :SIZE RT 120]
TRIHALF :SIZE/1.41
END
```

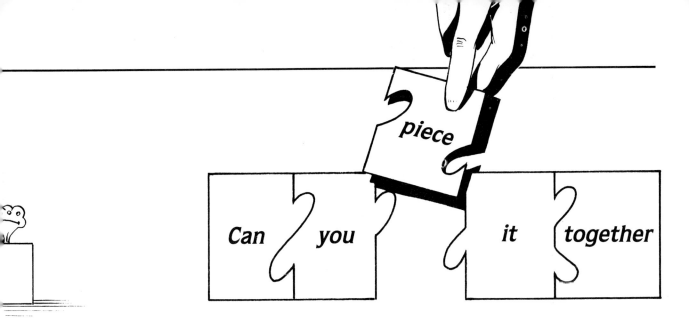

Can you *piece* it together

Below are 5 procedures. Put them in to the **ALPHABETLETTER** procedure in the right order and **ALPHABETLETTER** will draw a letter of the alphabet.

Alphabet letter
```
TO ALPHABETLETTER
PU SETPOS [-100 50] PD


END
```

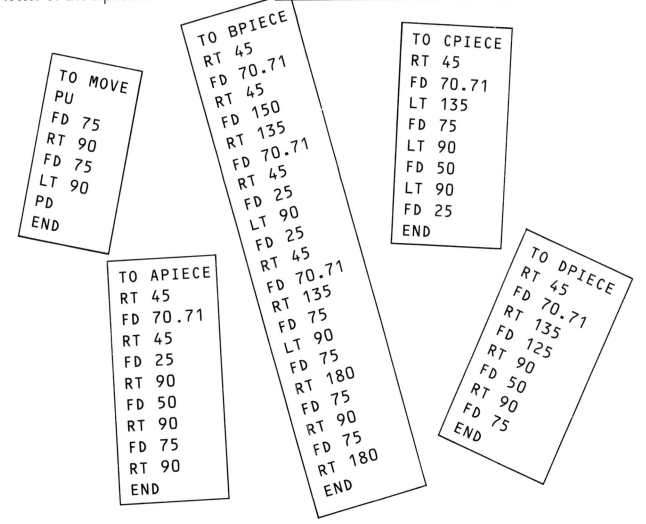

```
TO MOVE
PU
FD 75
RT 90
FD 75
LT 90
PD
END
```

```
TO BPIECE
RT 45
FD 70.71
RT 45
FD 150
RT 135
FD 70.71
RT 45
FD 25
LT 90
FD 25
RT 45
FD 70.71
RT 135
FD 75
LT 90
FD 75
RT 180
FD 75
RT 90
FD 75
RT 180
END
```

```
TO CPIECE
RT 45
FD 70.71
LT 135
FD 75
LT 90
FD 50
LT 90
FD 25
END
```

```
TO APIECE
RT 45
FD 70.71
RT 45
FD 25
RT 90
FD 50
RT 90
FD 75
RT 90
END
```

```
TO DPIECE
RT 45
FD 70.71
RT 135
FD 125
RT 90
FD 50
RT 90
FD 75
END
```

Messages

LOGO lets you program using words and lists.

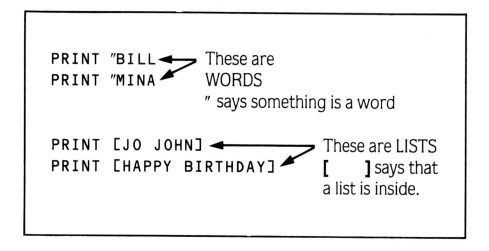

```
PRINT "BILL       These are
PRINT "MINA       WORDS
                  " says something is a word

PRINT [JO JOHN]          These are LISTS
PRINT [HAPPY BIRTHDAY]   [    ] says that
                         a list is inside.
```

You can print lists in procedures.
Write and edit your own letter.

I can only do one thing at a time. You can call me PR for short.

```
?TO LETTER
>PRINT [DEAR MUM]
>PRINT [DONT FORGET MY BIRTHDAY]
>PRINT [LOVE]
>PRINT [JEFF]
>END
```

No, it should be "LOVE not [LOVE]

Is Jane right?

```
?TO QUESTION :WORD
>PR [WHAT IS FRENCH FOR]
>PR :WORD
>END
```

```
?TO ANSWER :WD :FRWD
>PR [THE FRENCH FOR]
>PR :WD
>PR "IS
>PR :FRWD
>END
```

Jeff helped Jane write a party invitations procedure, but it has a bug.

```
TO INVITE :PERSON
PRINT "DEAR :PERSON
PRINT [YOU ARE INVITED TO A PARTY]
PRINT [LOVE FROM]
PRINT [JANE, JEFF, OGOL AND ORCIM]
END
```

The bug is in the line PRINT "DEAR :PERSON. The trouble is that "DEAR and :PERSON are both inputs and PRINT can only take one input at a time. The problem can be solved using SENTENCE which joins up 2 inputs and makes them into one input ready for PRINT. Try

```
TO FOOD :FRUIT
PR SE[MY FAVOURITE FOOD IS] :FRUIT
END
```

and

```
TO PALS :NAME
PR SE :NAME[IS MY BEST FRIEND]
END
```

I tie inputs together ready for PRINT *I'm* SE *for short.*

SENTENCE

Making friends

Jane wrote a procedure to print the names of her friends.

```
TO MYFRIENDS :FRIENDS
PRINT SE[MY BEST FRIENDS ARE] :FRIENDS
END
```

SE is short for sentence

```
?MAKE "FRIENDS [JONATHON
ANIL KAREN IAN NITA
GEHAN FRED RICHARD
ISABEL ETTA DONNA JO]
```

What happens if you leave out the : when using MAKE *boxes?*

Don't know. Let's try and find out.

"FRIENDS

MAKE makes a box in the computer's memory. It needs two inputs.
Input one is the name of the box.
Input two is the thing to go in the box.

1↴   2↴

MAKE "FRIENDS [ANIL KAREN]

MAKE *needs 2 inputs.*

Then, when you run the procedure MYFRIENDS or PRINT :FRIENDS LOGO will use whatever you've put in the FRIENDS box (the : tells LOGO to look in the box).

Make a Make Box

You will need some boxes, some sticky labels, pieces of card 2·5 cm by 25 cm (roughly) which will go in the boxes. Make a name for the box by writing a label and sticking it on.

Lists are written on the strips of card; one list goes in each box. For example, Jane's list of pets is

```
MAKE "PETS[CAT DOG TURTLE]
```

Label on the box   What's inside the box

Jane added a pair of dotty eyes to the box to remind her that LOGO needs dots to look inside. She needs to type
`PRINT :PETS` to check what is inside the box.

```
MAKE "MYCLASS[ANIL KATE ROBBO.....]
MAKE "FRUIT[ORANGE APPLE PLUM KIWI MANGO]
MAKE "TOPTWENTY [     ]
Try
PRINT :MYCLASS
PRINT :FRUIT
PRINT :TOPTWENTY
or
TO BESTFRIENDS :NAME
PRINT SE[MY BEST FRIENDS ARE] :NAME
PRINT SE[I HATE] :NAME
END
```

Jeff's super quiz for Ogol

I've set a question. Now I want to do three things.
1. *WAIT for Ogol to type a reply.*
2. *STORE the reply in the computer's memory.*
3. *TEST whether the reply is right or not.*

Procedures to debug

```
? To France
> Print [What is the
Capital of France?]
>
```

```
TO TABLES
PRINT [WHAT IS 5*4?]
MAKE "REPLY READLIST
IF REPLY =[20][PRINT "HOORAY][PRINT"BOO]
END
```

```
TO UN
PRINT [WHAT DO THE INITIALS U.N. STAND FOR?]
MAKE "REPLY READLIST
IF REPLY ="UNITED "NATIONS [PRINT[WELL DONE]][PRINT[BAD LUCK]]
END
```

```
TO MOUNT
PRINT [WHAT IS THE HIGHEST MOUNTAIN IN THE WORLD?]
MAKE REPLY READLIST
IF REPLY ="EVEREST [PRINT[YOURE RIGHT]][PRINT"UNLUCKY]
END
```

Readlist

READLIST is a LOGO word which reads what you type and puts it in a list. To STORE a reply, Jeff uses MAKE and READLIST together.

MAKE "REPLY READLIST

To TEST a reply use this kind of procedure.

TEST :REPLY = [PARIS]
IF TRUE [PRINT [WELL DONE]]
IF FALSE [PRINT [BAD LUCK]]

This tests to see if the reply is Paris. If it is, then the procedure prints 'Well done'. If it isn't, there is a 'bad luck' message. Try out the procedures below and debug them. Once debugged, they can be used to make a super quiz.

```
TO SUPERQUIZ
TABLES
UN
MOUNT
...
END
```

*It's not fair, it **is** Mount Everest.*

```
WHAT IS THE HIGHEST
MOUNTAIN IN THE WORLD?
MOUNT EVEREST
UNLUCKY
```

Ogol's answer EVEREST got a well done message. Can you fix MOUNT so that Jane gets one too.

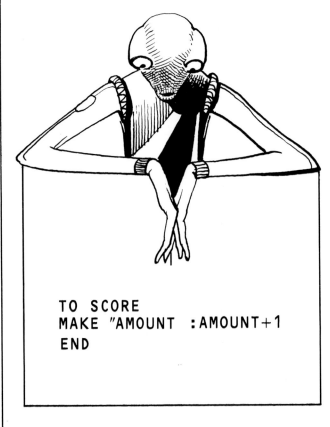

Orcim uses this procedure to keep score. Can you use it to keep track of the number of questions you get right? Your program could tell you after each answer how many you have scored.

```
TO SCORE
MAKE "AMOUNT :AMOUNT+1
END
```

Poem

That's not a bad poem.

I built it up 3 words at a time from lists.

Small cats laugh
Striped tigers jump
Short giraffes fly

Large red caterpillars wriggle fiercely on Wednesdays.

But what I'd really like to do is to choose the words for the poem at RANDOM.

```
MAKE "DOING
[RUN JUMP HOWL
FLY MOVE
>?
```

There's a procedure; CHOOSE that might help — CHOOSE picks things randomly from lists.

```
TO CHOOSE :LIST
OUTPUT ITEM (1+RANDOM COUNT :LIST) :LIST
END
```

CHOOSE is very useful even if you don't quite understand how it works to start with. To see how it works try these:

```
PRINT CHOOSE[A B C D E]
FD CHOOSE[10 20 30]
TYPE CHOOSE[ON IN BY AT]
TYPE CHOOSE :DOING
```

Limerick

There was a young turtle from _____
Who walked all day on a _____
It _____ in the night
And _____ in fright
And ended up in a _____

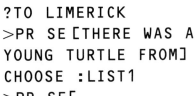

```
?TO LIMERICK
>PR SE[THERE WAS A
YOUNG TURTLE FROM]
CHOOSE :LIST1
>PR SE[
```

PR is short for PRINT
SE is short for SENTENCE
which ties 2 things together
ready for PRINT

**Experimenting
I hung the moon on various
Branches of the pine**

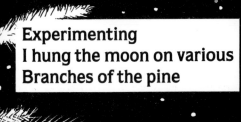

Make a poem with 17 beats.
The one above was written
by Hokushi. Try writing
your own with help from
LOGO.

First things first

First

Try

```
?PRINT FIRST[ONE TWO THREE]
```

Butfirst

What do you think the computer will reply to these commands?

```
PRINT FIRST[A B C D E]
PRINT BUTLAST[TREE FLOWER BUSH]
PRINT LAST[MON TUES WED THURS FRI]

PRINT BUTFIRST "ABRACADABRA
PRINT BUTLAST "OGOL
PRINT BUTLAST[SHE SELLS SEASHELLS]
```

Try them out

```
?MAKE "CLASS[ANN MARTIN
PETRA SAM MIKE CLARE
CAROL RICHARD KAREN
JULI STEVEN ANDREW
LIZ]
```

The butfirst game

1. Make a list of people in your class and type it into the computer.
2. Tear a sheet of paper into strips and write one name on each strip.
3. Put them in a box (you can use a **MAKE** box).
4. Close your eyes and pick a name.
5. You win (at least stay alive) if you can get the computer to pick out the name from the computer list using

   FIRST
   BUTFIRST
   LAST
   BUTLAST

   Fail and you lose a life. You have 3 lives.

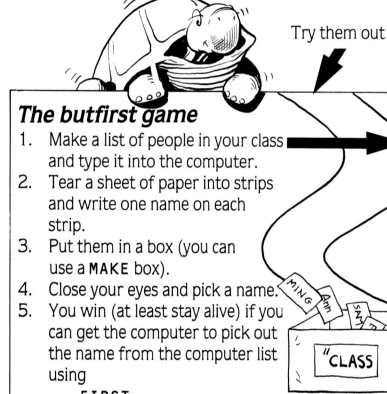

```
PRINT LAST BUTLAST
BUTLAST :CLASS
```

Jeff's version of the **BUTFIRST** game is harder. He asked Jane to pick bits of words using **FIRST** etc.

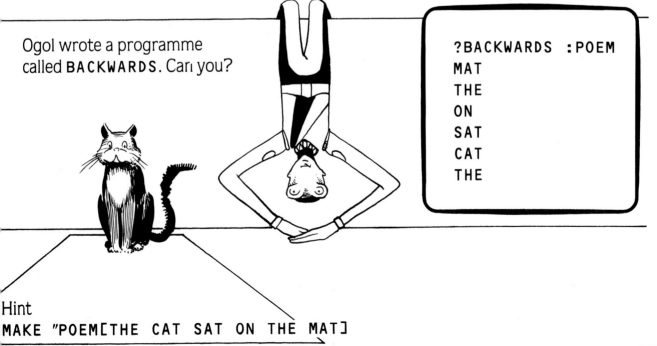

Ogol wrote a programme called **BACKWARDS**. Can you?

```
?BACKWARDS :POEM
MAT
THE
ON
SAT
CAT
THE
```

Hint
`MAKE "POEM[THE CAT SAT ON THE MAT]`

Party time

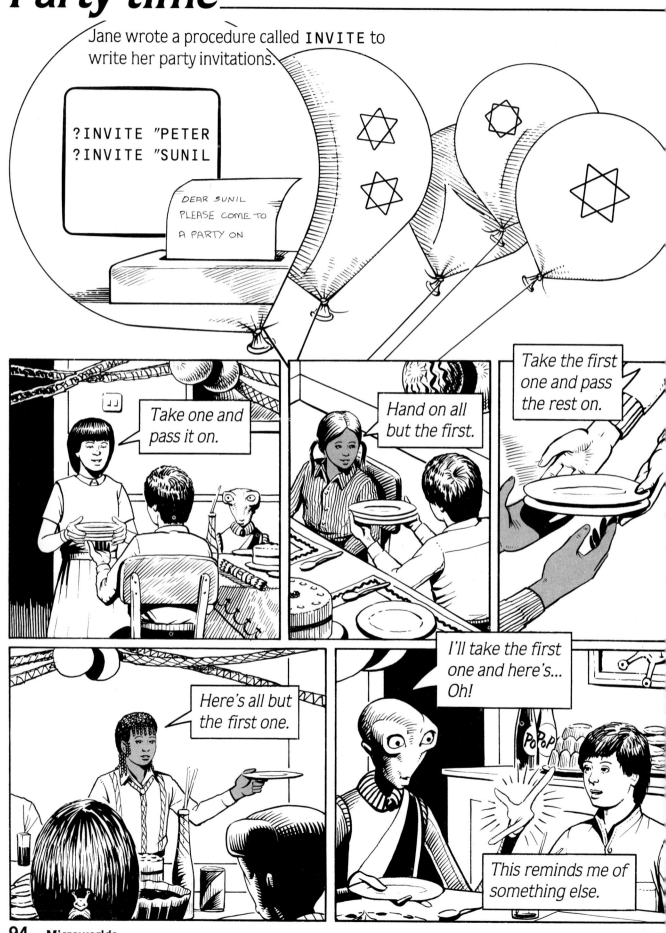

Jane wrote a procedure called INVITE to write her party invitations.

?INVITE "PETER
?INVITE "SUNIL

DEAR SUNIL
PLEASE COME TO
A PARTY ON

Take one and pass it on.

Hand on all but the first.

Take the first one and pass the rest on.

Here's all but the first one.

I'll take the first one and here's... Oh!

This reminds me of something else.

Jane made a list of everyone she wanted to invite to the party and then INVITEd them one at a time.

```
MAKE "FRIENDS [.............]
```

```
INVITE FIRST :FRIEND
INVITE FIRST BUTFIRST :FRIEND
INVITE FIRST BUTFIRST BUTFIRST :FRIEND
```

Jeff used the pattern to write a PARTY procedure which would work even if they had a hundred friends.

But it's got a pattern.

It's a long list.

So we have to tell it to STOP if it runs out.

```
TO PARTY :PEOPLE
INVITE FIRST :PEOPLE
PARTY BUTFIRST :PEOPLE
END
```

Like we ran out of plates.

There's a bug — it's run out of people.

Try writing a procedure which makes words into a triangle.

```
?TRIWORD "SAUSAGES

SAUSAGES
SAUSAGE
SAUSAG
SAUSA
SAUS
SAU
SA
S
```

Over to you.

Charts is a fine thing

Jeff wanted to compare the heights of people in his class.

```
TO BAR :UP :ALONG
REPEAT 2 [FD :UP RT 90
FD :ALONG RT 90]
END
```

Try
```
BAR 20 5
BAR 5 20
BAR 100 10
```

What happens with
```
BAR 0 50
BAR 50 0
```

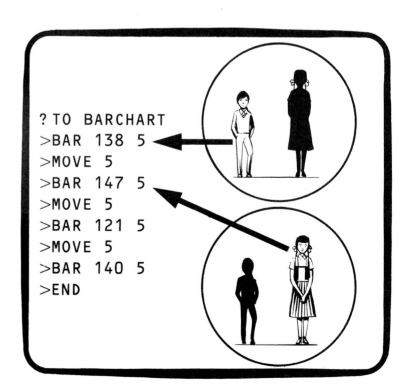

```
? TO BARCHART
>BAR 138 5
>MOVE 5
>BAR 147 5
>MOVE 5
>BAR 121 5
>MOVE 5
>BAR 140 5
>END
```

But BARCHART *takes ages to type. Ogol wants to chart the whole of the class.*

1 Make a list.
MAKE "HEIGHTS [138 147 121]
The list can be as long as you like. Don't forget the square bracket at the end.

2 Use the list in a procedure – like FASTBARCHART. The second line of that procedure means the procedure will stop when all the numbers in the list have been used and the list is empty.

```
TO FASTBARCHART :LIST
IF :LIST = [ ][STOP]
BAR (FIRST :LIST) 5
MOVE 5
FASTBARCHART BUTFIRST :LIST
END
```

3 Now try typing something like
FASTBARCHART :HEIGHTS
There are other uses!

TOP OF THE GALACTIC POPS	
1	ZUGLUGAZUG
2	SUZI & THE BLEEPERS
3	WUZZGOP
4	YIL POP QUIRK
5	THE QUARKS
6	✳ ₷ᘈᕼᘔᎶᑌᕎ
7	GRIIIIIPPS

Secret codes

```
TO CODE :WOTSIT
PRINT WORD(BF :WOTSIT) (FIRST :WOTSIT)
END
```

Print all but the first letter

Print the first letter

ELLOH

BUTFIRST and **FIRST** are used to cut a word up and move the bits around. **WORD** sticks the bits together ready for **PRINT**.

There are many ways to use **FIRST**, **BUTFIRST**, **LAST** and **BUTLAST** to write codes (with a bit of help from **WORD**). Try writing a **CODE2** procedure which can change rubbish into hrubbis. Or a **CODE3** procedure which can turn twins into swint and word into dorw.

```
TO CODELIST :LISTOFWORDS
IF :LISTOFWORDS = [ ][STOP]
CODE FIRST :LISTOFWORDS
CODELIST :BF :LISTOFWORDS
END
```

SSSS HHH

ETS AKE
NOTHER ODE
AN KEE I
SECRE

But I don't know what the missing letter is. It could be bets, lets or almost anything.

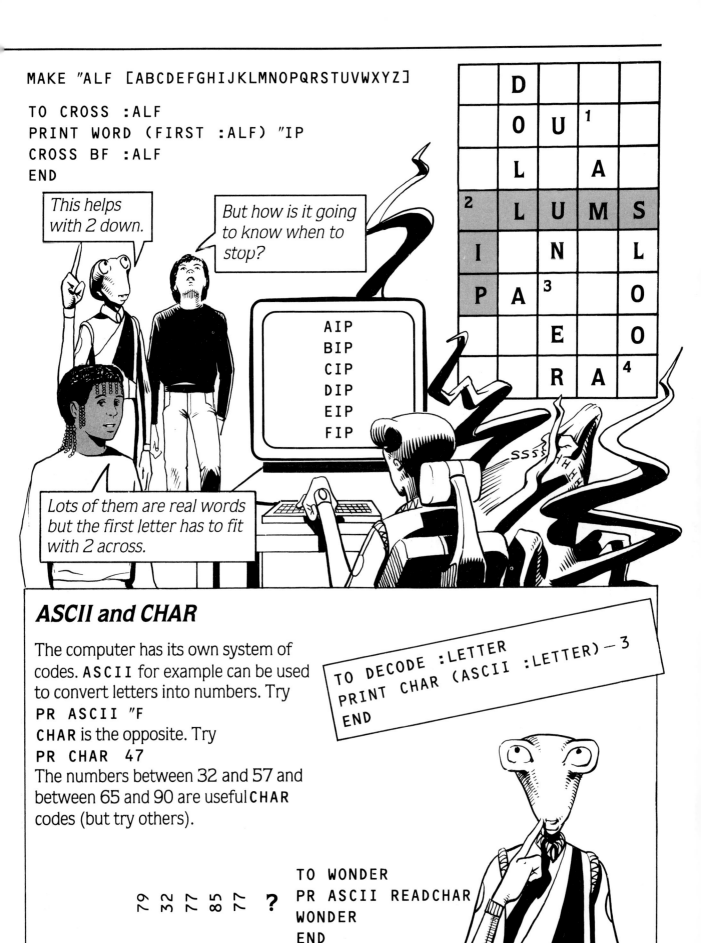

```
MAKE "ALF [ABCDEFGHIJKLMNOPQRSTUVWXYZ]

TO CROSS :ALF
PRINT WORD (FIRST :ALF) "IP
CROSS BF :ALF
END
```

This helps with 2 down.

But how is it going to know when to stop?

```
AIP
BIP
CIP
DIP
EIP
FIP
```

Lots of them are real words but the first letter has to fit with 2 across.

Crossword grid:

	D			
	O	U	1	
	L	A		
2 L	U	M	S	
I	N		L	
P	A	3	O	
	E		O	
	R	A	4	

ASCII and CHAR

The computer has its own system of codes. `ASCII` for example can be used to convert letters into numbers. Try

`PR ASCII "F`

`CHAR` is the opposite. Try

`PR CHAR 47`

The numbers between 32 and 57 and between 65 and 90 are useful `CHAR` codes (but try others).

```
TO DECODE :LETTER
PRINT CHAR (ASCII :LETTER) - 3
END
```

79 32 77 85 77 ?

```
TO WONDER
PR ASCII READCHAR
WONDER
END
```

Eht slasrever emag

The reversals game

```
TO REVERSE :CODE
IF :CODE = " [OUTPUT " ]
OUTPUT WORD REVERSE BF :CODE FIRST :CODE
END
```

The players all have the script above. When they start to read their part, they stand up. They can't sit down until they reach **END** This is what happened when Ogol and friends played the Reversal Game with the word PART. Try the game yourself with a longer word and more friends. (**BF** is short for **BUTFIRST**; " is word with no letters left in it; and **WORD** joins two words together.)

1

2

3 *I'll join P on to the* **REVERSE** *of* "ART. *Your turn.*

4 *I'll join A on to the* **REVERSE** *of* "RT. *Your turn.*

5 *I'll join R on to the* **REVERSE** *of* "T. *Your turn.*

6 *And I'll join T on to the* **REVERSE** *of* "

7 *The* **REVERSE** *of blank is blank.*

```
PRINT  REVERSE  "HELLO
PRINT  REVERSE  "ABRACADABRA
PRINT  REVERSE  REVERSE  "SAUSAGES
```

WANTED
The longest palindrome
in the English language.

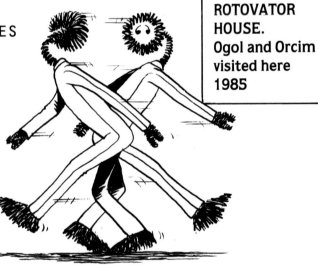

ROTOVATOR
HOUSE.
Ogol and Orcim
visited here
1985

```
TO MAKEPAL :WD
PRINT WORD :WD (REVERSE :WD)
END
```
Try something like
MAKEPAL :RHUBARB.
and you'll get
RHUBARBBRABUHR

Try these:
MAKEPAL works with numbers.
MAKEPAL 139 will give 139931
Try dividing the result by 11 —
and see what happens.
Not all palindromes have a double
letter in the middle. Edit
MAKEPAL so that the last
letter isn't doubled.
MAKEPAL2 would produce
RHUBARBRABUHR

LOGO ideas

Introduction

LOGO is a computer language built up out of just a few key ideas. We have made a list of some of the most important ones below. There is no special order to these, though some ideas are easier than others. You certainly won't need all these ideas at once. *Remember*: driving your turtle across the floor (or moving it across the screen) is programming your computer just as much as inventing the most complicated LOGO program. You are the only person who can decide what program to write and when you want to learn more.

Gaining control of the system

Programming a computer is fun. It puts you in charge. There are lots of ways you can get started. You can use a floor turtle (pages 6 and 7) or you can draw over your screen on a see-through sheet (page 7). You can play turtle (page 12) or you can switch on your LOGO eyes (page 13). You can look things up in your manual (or this book) or ask a friend. You can even keep a LOGO diary if you like.

Using repeat

Using the REPEAT command is one way to make LOGO do things over and over again. Repeating the simplest or 'buggiest' idea can produce spectacular patterns (pages 14-19). When you're solving problems, keep open a LOGO eye for repeatable ideas. Pages 34, 38, 43 and 46 are some of the pages using REPEAT.

Defining a procedure

Procedures are ideas you use to teach LOGO pages 20-5). There are two ways to think about procedures. First, a procedure is a building block. It is something LOGO will do as many times as you ask it to. Secondly, a procedure is a list of commands that fit together. The commands can all be made to happen just by using the name of the procedure. Sometimes you will just need to understand how it works, especially when you are debugging.

Don't forget: LOGO will forget all the procedures you have defined when you switch off the computer, unless you have saved them (page 29).

Editing a procedure lets you debug it, change it, see how it works or just play around with it (pages 26-8).

Using subprocedures

When you use a procedure inside another one, you're making it into a subprocedure (pages 32-5). Using subprocedures is a good way to solve tricky problems. Try to break up a difficult problem into easier bits and then define a subprocedure for each bit (pages 36 and 40-1). Choose an easy bit to start with. Of course, if any of the bits is too complicated, you can always break it down into smaller subprocedures (pages 42-3).

Using inputs

Using inputs in a procedure lets you use just one procedure to do lots of different things (pages 44-5). For example, inputs let you vary how much to turn (an input to RT or LT, pages 46-7), how far to go (an input to FD or BK, pages 48-9), how many repeats (pages 50-1), or to vary the colour (pages 52-3). You can even let the computer choose its own input using RANDOM (pages 52-5).

Using recursion

The idea of recursion is to use a procedure as a subprocedure of itself (page 60). Recursion is like the story of the genie who offered 3 wishes. If you're crafty, your third wish ought to be to ask for 3 more wishes!

You can use recursion just like a repeat, to make things happen over and over again (pages 64-7). Recursion can also be used in other ways. It can be used for counting (pages 74-5), for spiral patterns (pages 70-1 and 76-7), for poetry (pages 90-1) and for party invitations (pages 94-5).

Using conditionals

There are two ways of making LOGO ask itself a question. The first is by using IF (pages 72-3). The second is by using TEST. They are very similar. Test if something is true. If it is, do this; if it is not, do that.

Using lists

Lists are collections of words and numbers. All lists live in square brackets and anything in square brackets is a list. Lists are LOGO's way of keeping track of what to do. For example, REPEAT 10 [A LIST OF THINGS TO DO] (pages 14-19), lists of friends (pages 86 and 94-5) or secret codes (pages 98-9). Lists often have to be used with recursion which involves us all in a new way of thinking (pages 100-1).

Backword

This is a book about ideas not a LOGO manual. Just as people speak different dialects of English, so there are lots of different dialects of LOGO. In fact there are at least 10 dialects for the computers you are likely to see at home or at school. Unless you are very lucky, you will find that some of the LOGO words inside this book and some of the key presses (e.g. CTRL and G) won't work on your computer. Don't worry – it's the ideas that count. Use your manual, your friends, your sister or brother or even your teacher. Someone will probably be able to help – if not, try everything! You can't break LOGO!

Index